A NOTE TO PARENTS
FROM FOCUS ON THE FAMILY

Adventures in Odyssey's "Passages" series has been designed to retell Bible stories in such a new and creative way that young readers will be able to experience them as if for the first time.

All the "Passages" novels are based squarely on key episodes of scriptural history. Anyone who is intimately acquainted with the Bible will recognize the basic outlines and spiritual lessons of the stories. But the names have been changed, the details have been altered, and (most importantly) the settings have been shifted to the land of *Marus*—an exciting world accidentally "discovered" by a group of kids from Odyssey.

Why this fictional device? Because familiarity can dull the impact of an oft-told tale. By "dressing up" the biblical stories in a new set of "clothes," we hope to release their inherent power in new ways . . . and change young lives in the process.

This strategy didn't originate with "Passages." C. S. Lewis did exactly the same thing when he wrote *The Chronicles of Narnia.* Narnia was born when Lewis came to the realization that fantasy can be a particularly powerful tool for communicating gospel truths. "By casting all these things into an imaginary world," he once wrote, "stripping them of their stained-glass and Sunday school associations, one could make them for the first time appear in their real potency" (from Lewis's essay "Sometimes Fairy Stories May Say Best What's to Be Said"). This is exactly what we are trying to do with "Passages."

Parents should also be aware that, consistent with similar elements in the biblical accounts, these books contain occasional scenes of supernatural activity.

As has always been the case with *Adventures in Odyssey,* we sincerely hope that parents and children will read and discuss the "Passages" novels *together.* That's the best way to avoid misunderstanding.

PASSAGES™

Fendar's Legacy

Paul McCusker

Thomas Nelson Inc
Nashville

FENDAR'S LEGACY

Copyright © 2000 by Focus on the Family. All rights reserved. International copyright secured.

Library of Congress Cataloging-in-Publication Data requested.

ISBN 1-56179-845-2

A Focus on the Family book published in Nashville, Tennessee, by Tommy Nelson™, a division of Thomas Nelson, Inc.

The author is represented by the literary agency of Alive Communications, 1465 Kelly Johnson Blvd., Suite 320, Colorado Springs, CO 80920.

This is a work of fiction, and any resemblance between the characters in this book and real persons is coincidental.

Editor: Larry K. Weeden
Front cover design: Peak Creative Group

Printed in the United States of America

00 01 02 03 04 QPV 10 9 8 7 6 5 4 3 2 1

for R⸳ ky, James, and E⸳

Adventures in Odyssey Presents
Passages, Book VI

PROLOGUE

John Avery Whittaker, or Whit as he was best known around
Odyssey, turned on his windshield wipers. The snow was
falling heavily this morning, as if it were trying to make up for
lost time after yesterday's sunshine. He slowed down and
squinted at the road ahead. The turnoff for Hillingdale Haven
was coming up.

He ran his fingers through his mop of white hair. He felt
tired. He hadn't slept well last night, and a morning spent in
front of the microfilm machine at the library was, at best, dizzying.

Whit and his good friend Jack Allen had been trying to tie
up the loose ends of their investigation of the Marus manuscripts, a collection of stories about kids who'd supposedly
slipped from Odyssey to another world called Marus. From the
very first manuscript, which Jack had found in an old trunk
belonging to a dead teacher named Maude McCutcheon, the
two men had been hooked. They'd had to find out more. So
they had followed a trail that led to more manuscripts and,
finally, to a man named James Curtis. He'd written the stories
over the past 70 years.

When Whit and Jack visited him for the first time yesterday, James had not only insisted that the stories about Marus

were true, but also that he'd gone to Marus himself. He hoped that he might somehow return to Marus now that he was an old man.

Ultimately, Whit and Jack didn't know what to believe. It didn't help that James lived at Hillingdale Haven, an institution outside Odyssey for those with emotional and mental problems.

Whit and Jack had talked about it late into the night and at the library this morning. They had hoped to find a clue they had missed in the stories of Anna and Kyle, Wade Mullens, and the other kids who had gone to Marus and returned. And then there was Scott Graham, who James Curtis claimed had gone to Marus and stayed there. Unfortunately, none of them could be found to verify the stories.

All the evidence fell right on the edge of plausibility. If you believed that other worlds existed, the evidence pointed to the possibility that those kids really had gone to Marus. If you didn't believe in other worlds, the evidence was circumstantial and didn't prove anything at all.

In the end, Jack couldn't accept that Marus was real. "James Curtis is an imaginative writer who mixed fact with fiction to come up with his stories. That's all," he concluded.

Whit shook his head wearily but understood Jack's feelings. "I wish I knew what to think" was all Whit could say to his friend. Could other worlds exist, with God somehow working in them similarly to how He works in ours? Or had James Curtis and Maude McCutcheon created an elaborate fantasy that they had begun to believe was real?

Whit and Jack had parted company so they could get on with their work. On the way back to his soda shop/discovery emporium called Whit's End, Whit had decided to pay James Curtis one more visit. *Even if the manuscripts are fiction, they're still good stories,* Whit reasoned. *If James will let me, I'll put them in the library at Whit's End for kids to read.*

That's how Whit came to find himself turning into the driveway for Hillingdale Haven in a heavy snowfall. As he parked his car and dashed for the front door of the massive, red-stone complex, he noticed a police car sitting along the curb. Inside the reception area, a police officer was talking with a doctor Whit knew from one of the many civic groups to which he belonged. It was Dr. Jennings. The officer's black leather coat contrasted starkly with the doctor's white smock, Whit thought. He walked to the front desk and asked the receptionist if he could see James Curtis.

The woman looked at him awkwardly, then called out, "Dr. Jennings? This man wants to visit James Curtis."

The doctor recognized Whit immediately and came over. "Whit! What are you doing here?" he asked.

"I had hoped to see James Curtis."

The officer followed the doctor and inquired of Whit, "You know him?"

"I met him yesterday," Whit replied. "Why? Is something wrong?"

The doctor looked stressed. "No. There's nothing wrong," he answered nervously. "Why would anything be wrong?"

"You need to relax, Doc," the officer said. "We'll find him."

"James Curtis is missing?" Whit asked, astonished.

Dr. Jennings was a slight man with a birdlike face and thinning hair. He rubbed his eyes. "Nobody knows how it happened. He was in his room at bedtime, happy as could be. When he didn't come down for breakfast at his usual time, they checked his room. He was gone."

"It's a big building. Are you sure he isn't around somewhere?" the officer suggested.

"We have doctors and nurses on staff around the clock. They monitor the halls. We've even checked the videotapes from the security cameras. He didn't leave his room."

"Obviously he did," the officer observed.

"This is really peculiar," the doctor whined. "We've never lost a patient like this. Never!"

"So why were you here to see him?" the officer asked Whit.

"I wanted to continue our conversation from yesterday," he replied.

"What were you talking about?"

"Some stories James wrote. I've been very interested in them."

The officer grunted as if deciding that Whit was irrelevant

to the case and turned to Dr. Jennings. "Come on, Doc. I need to write out a full report and call it in."

Dr. Jennings nodded, and the two men walked away.

"He's not dangerous, is he?" Whit heard the policeman ask.

"Oh, heavens, no!" the doctor replied as they disappeared around a corner.

Unsure what to do next, Whit was about to go back to his car when he became aware of someone at his elbow. He turned to face a man with dark, curly hair and a neatly trimmed, graying beard. The man clutched a package under the arm of his thick overcoat.

"You're a friend of James Curtis?" the man asked Whit.

"An acquaintance," Whit corrected.

"You said something about stories that James Curtis wrote," the man continued.

"That's right," Whit affirmed. "But who are you?"

The man flashed a press badge. "I'm a reporter for the *National Church Times*. I was supposed to meet Mr. Curtis this morning to talk."

Whit pointed at the large, brown envelope under the man's arm. "Is that what I think it is?"

The reporter glanced down at the package, then back at Whit with a half smile. "You tell me."

"My guess is that it's an old-fashioned school notebook containing a story about a place called Marus."

The reporter nodded. "That's right. Mr. Curtis had sent it to me to read, and I was bringing it back. I wanted to talk to him. But now he's gone."

"So it seems."

"How does someone disappear from a closely watched room?" The reporter kept his eyes on Whit.

Whit shrugged.

"You know about Marus," the reporter said.

"Only recently."

"Then I think we should talk." The reporter turned to the receptionist and asked, "Is there somewhere around here we can get a hot drink?"

She pointed upward and replied, "There's a café next floor up."

The café turned out to be a small room with vending machines. Whit and the reporter got coffee and sat down at a table in the corner.

"What's your interest in James Curtis?" Whit asked.

"I write articles about unexplained phenomena," the reporter replied as he sipped, then winced at, his coffee.

"What kind of phenomena?"

"Sightings of angels, claims of miraculous healings, that sort of thing," he said casually. "James Curtis had read my articles in the paper and contacted me about Marus. Then he sent me this story to read." The reporter placed his hand on the brown envelope.

"May I see it?" Whit asked.

"After you tell me what you know about it," he answered.

"That's fair," Whit said with a smile. And for the next 20 minutes, he explained to the reporter how he'd come to know about the manuscripts through Jack Allen and how their trail had led them to James Curtis.

The reporter handed the package over. Whit pulled a familiar-looking black school notebook from the envelope. On the first page was written: *Chronicle of the Delivered*. It was dated June 4, 1998. "I haven't seen this one," Whit said.

"I'd like to see some of the others you mentioned. Did Mr. Curtis keep any in his room?"

"I think so."

They finished their coffee and went back down to the reception area. Dr. Jennings was in his office, looking even more stressed and nervous once he found out that Whit was with a reporter. "I don't want any publicity over this," the doctor insisted.

"I'm not here about that," the reporter assured him. "I'm here about Mr. Curtis's stories. Mr. Whittaker seems to think he kept a few of them in his room."

"Everything's in his room, just as it was," the doctor stated. "He didn't take anything with him."

"I assume he has relatives who'll come—"

The doctor shook his head quickly. "No living relatives. He

had two sisters who died in the past couple of years. That's all. So I don't know what we'll do if . . . if . . ."

"You can't find him?" the reporter said, finishing the doctor's sentence.

"Oh, we'll find him," Dr. Jennings said in a tight voice. "People don't just disappear off the face of the earth. We'll find him."

"It would be helpful if we could see the manuscripts. May we go to his room?" Whit asked.

The doctor hesitated.

"There may be a clue in them about where he went," Whit added.

Dr. Jennings thought about it for a moment. "All right, but it's strictly off-the-record," he finally said. "I don't want any press about this. What will people think of Hillingdale Haven if they find out our patients can simply vanish like that?"

Satisfied, Whit and the reporter got up to leave.

"Don't take anything," Dr. Jennings warned.

The two men agreed that they wouldn't.

"Mrs. Delullo will accompany you," Dr. Jennings said, nodding to a nurse who sat at a desk nearby. She got up immediately and began to fumble for some keys.

On the way to the room, the reporter asked Whit, "Do you think people can disappear from this world?"

Whit cocked an eyebrow. "You're really asking if I think James Curtis has gone back to Marus, right?"

"I suppose I am."

"I don't know," Whit replied candidly. "I honestly don't know."

Mrs. Delullo opened the door to James Curtis's room and stood next to it like a guard. The room was exactly as Whit had seen it the day before. Two large, wood-framed windows gave a view of the grounds; snow covered everything now. A small fireplace stood along one of the walls, and a sink stood in a corner.

"It's like stepping back into the Victorian age," the reporter said as he looked around. "A four-poster bed, the mahogany writing table, the old-fashioned chairs . . ."

"This front part of Hillingdale Haven was built over a hundred years ago," Mrs. Delullo said.

The reporter whistled through his teeth. "Just look at that woodwork along the ceiling and the door. They don't make them like this anymore."

As he had the day before, Whit noticed a collection of newspapers scattered on a small coffee table. He now saw that several of them were copies of the *National Church Times*. "An avid reader," Whit said, pointing.

The reporter smiled.

Whit went to the writing desk and looked around. In the

center were a ring of keys, an empty coffee mug, several fountain pens, and a roll of tape. A short stack of files and papers
sat off to one side. Whit didn't feel he had the right to dig very
deep, but he hoped a copy of one of the manuscripts might be
seen easily. He found two sitting in the stack: the story about
Annison and another about Draven.

"Do you think Dr. Jennings would mind if we stayed here
and read these?" the reporter asked Mrs. Delullo.

"I'll have to ask," she said.

The reporter slid down onto one of the wing-backed chairs
with the two manuscripts. "We'll wait here while you do," he
said, getting comfortable. Mrs. Delullo seemed to disapprove of
his impudence, but she turned and walked off. Dr. Jennings
must have given his okay, because after that Mrs. Delullo
returned only now and then to make sure the door was open
and the two men were behaving.

Still clutching the manuscript the reporter had given him,
Whit sat down in the desk chair.

A clock ticked on the mantle above the fireplace. Apart
from that and the sound of turning pages, the room was silent.
Whit thought he could hear the snow falling. He opened the
school notebook and began to read.

CHAPTER ONE

◆━━━━━━◆

"Look at that!" Michelle Brewer exclaimed from behind the bushes.

Danny Taylor grabbed her arm and pulled her down. "Get down!" he demanded. "Are you trying to get us in trouble?"

"Ouch!" Michelle said and rubbed her arm. "Don't ever lay a hand on me again, you male chauvinist!"

"What?" Danny asked, not sure what she'd said but suspecting from her tone that it wasn't nice.

"You heard me." She glared at him through her glasses.

Danny grunted and peered through the bush toward Trickle Lake. Though it was midafternoon on a hot summer's day, a bonfire raged along the shore. Dozens of teenagers—maybe even hundreds, Danny thought—were milling around the lake and in the nearby forest. Tents had been set up around the various campsites and picnic tables. Loud rock music blasted through a sound system that had been set up by the dock. A peculiar smell filled the air.

It was June 1968, and this was a music festival spontaneously arranged by a group from nearby Campbell Community College. Word had gone around to Odyssey's teens, and somehow Michelle had heard about it. Danny wasn't surprised. Michelle somehow heard about *everything*, whether she was supposed to or not.

The crowd of young people had started to gather at Trickle Lake around noon. Most of them were students, with long hair and Day-Glo headbands, psychedelic jewelry and tie-dye shirts, bell-bottoms and sandals, and peace signs and radical placards.

"I told you they were going to have a festival today," Michelle gloated. "Didn't I tell you?"

To be honest, Danny didn't much like Michelle. She was bossy and talked a lot and had to have everything her own way. She was the kind of girl who annoyed all the boys and got on the nerves of all the girls. Mostly her opinions got her into trouble. She always complained about how men were Neanderthals who oppressed women and said that one day women would rule the universe so they could truly be free. Danny figured Michelle expected to be the president when that happened.

So why was Danny with her now? He had no choice. Michelle was his cousin, and his parents expected him to be her friend when she came to visit, which she did every summer as soon as school was out.

Danny got the impression that Michelle was sent to them because everybody else was too preoccupied to deal with her. Michelle's mother was in Cleveland, busy running a political campaign for a seat in Congress. ("Summer is a hectic campaigning time," he'd heard her say.) And Michelle's father, who lived with his new wife in Seattle, was too busy with his new family. So it became Danny's chore to keep Michelle entertained and out of his parents' hair.

Today he had thought they were going to go play at McCalister Park, but then she had sprung this idea on him right after they had left the house.

"There's a big hippie festival up at Trickle Lake," she had said. "Wouldn't it be groovy to see it?"

"No," Danny had replied honestly.

"I want to see it!" Danny's younger brother, Wayne, had chimed in.

But Danny had snapped at Wayne to go home. It was bad

enough having to put up with Michelle. He didn't want his little brother tagging along, too.

Wayne had pouted and gone back to the porch.

Michelle had then ignored both Danny and Wayne, climbed on her bike, and taken off in the direction of Trickle Lake. Danny had leaped onto his bike and gone after her. The entire way up, he had argued with her until he was breathless. He had said they would get into trouble. He had said the students would yell at them for being there. It had been no use. He had thought about turning around and letting her go on her own, but he knew his parents would blame him if they got home from work and anything had happened to her.

"That's the life," Michelle said now, gesturing to the hippies from behind the bushes. "Freedom to do whatever you want, whenever you want. When women are in charge, this is how it'll be."

Danny wasn't impressed. It looked like nothing more than a big cookout. His family had them all the time, but without the long hair, loud music, and weird clothes.

A twig snapped behind them. Danny and Michelle spun around. Wayne stood there with an impish grin on his face.

"What are you doing here?" Danny cried out in a harsh whisper.

"Mom and Dad didn't want me to be home alone, remember?" Wayne responded, sounding like a smart aleck.

"You're 10 years old. You know how to be home alone."

"But Mom said—"

"Oh, be quiet and get down before somebody sees you!" Michelle snapped.

Wayne stooped down and crab-crawled over to them. "What's going on?" he asked as he tried to squeeze between them to see.

Danny frowned. "Nothing," he said disgustedly. "It's boring. Let's go home."

"Not yet," Michelle said. "You know what? I think it's safe."

"Safe? Safe to do what?" Danny asked.

Michelle started to crawl around the bush.

"What are you doing?" Danny asked, his voice rising in pitch.

"I want to mingle."

"Mingle! Are you nuts? They don't want some *girl* hanging around."

"They won't care. They're too laid-back to care." She came out from behind the bush and stood up, then took a scarf out of her back pocket and tied it around her mop of black hair. She adjusted her glasses on her freckled nose and stepped confidently toward the lake.

"I don't believe it!" Danny said with a groan.

Michelle wandered in and out of the clusters of students who were drinking out of cans or nibbling from bags of food they'd brought. No one seemed to notice her.

"She's right," Wayne said. "Nobody cares."

"That's only because it's so crowded."

"Then we can go look around, too," Wayne suggested. "It's going to get even more crowded pretty soon."

"No, we're staying—" Danny stopped in midsentence because something about what Wayne had just said caused him to think twice. "Wayne, what do you mean it's going to get more crowded?"

"Because of all the police cars."

"*What* police cars?" Danny asked, a sick feeling growing in his stomach.

"The ones I saw driving up when I was following you. They would have beat me here if I hadn't cut cross-country."

Danny grabbed his brother's shirt. "The police are coming? Why didn't you say something?"

Wayne shrugged. "I wanted to see them bust everybody."

"But if they bust everybody, they'll bust *us*, too!"

"Oh," Wayne said. "I didn't think of that."

Danny scrambled to his feet. "You stay here," he ordered. "I'll go get Michelle."

Feeling about as conspicuous as an elephant at a party of pink flamingos, Danny made his way down to the small dock, which was the last place he'd seen Michelle. The music blasted through the speakers and pounded his head. A gruff voice sang about going on a magic carpet ride.

Danny felt a tug at his sleeve.

"You're going in the wrong direction," Wayne said and pointed. "She's over there."

"I told you to wait behind the bush!" Danny shouted at his brother.

"But you were going in the wrong direction," Wayne offered in his defense.

Danny pulled at his brother's arm. "Stay close to me."

No one seemed to notice them. The students had all gathered in small clusters, where they were chatting about things like the Vietnam War, a place called Berkeley, the Democratic Party convention in Chicago, and other things Danny didn't understand. A few sat around guitar players and smoked strange-looking cigarettes. Unlike Michelle, who talked constantly about what a great life she thought this was, Danny didn't like this party at all.

"Where is she?" he muttered irritably—and then walked right into her.

"Watch where you're going!" she shouted at him over the music. She adjusted her glasses and scarf and then fingered a necklace of beads.

Danny pointed at the necklace. "Where did you get that?" he asked loudly.

"That lady in the tent over there gave it to me." Michelle gestured broadly.

Danny glanced at the tent, where a young woman in a peasant dress and bright smile sat and offered homemade goods to whoever passed by.

"That's what I'd like to do," Michelle said into Danny's ear. "Be free all day and make things in a tent."

"Right now we have to get out of here!" Danny called over the blaring music. "The police are on their way!"

"What?" Michelle asked, tipping her ear toward Danny.

Danny spoke louder. "I said, the police are coming!"

A young man with a long mustache and granny glasses suddenly turned to Danny. "Did you say the cops are coming?" he asked.

"Yeah."

"I saw them first," Wayne added.

The young man turned quickly to the group he'd been talking to and yelled, "Cops!"

The word shot like cannon fire around that group and then to other groups, and suddenly there was a wild commotion as the students threw down their cigarettes and scrambled for the trees. A whistle blew from somewhere and then another from somewhere else, and the police swarmed in, their dark-blue uniforms a strange contrast to the surroundings. The music abruptly stopped, the sound replaced with shouts from the police and the students. An officer with a megaphone announced something about this being an illegal assembly and for everyone to stop where they were. No one did.

"My folks are gonna kill us! We've gotta get out of here!" Danny yelled. But there was nowhere to run. The police had moved in from all sides, and Danny, Michelle, and Wayne found themselves squeezed onto the small, wooden dock that reached out into the lake.

"The boats," Michelle said. There were small boats at the end of the dock, and she raced toward them. She seemed to think they could escape by paddling away. Confused about what to do, Danny and Wayne followed her. The three of them reached the ladder that led down to the boats. A crush of people, all with the same idea, arrived seconds behind them. Unfortunately, the back of the crowd didn't stop when the front of the crowd reached the end of the dock. Soon people were being pushed into the lake. Danny saw Michelle go head over heels into the water. In the next instant, he and Wayne were forced in, too.

Danny was a good swimmer and quickly pushed his way to the surface. He looked around for Wayne and Michelle but had a hard time seeing. Water was pouring down onto him from somewhere above, as if he'd come up under a waterfall. *But there's no waterfall at Trickle Lake*, he remembered, *so what's this falling on my head?* He kicked to get away from the annoying splashing but found that his feet touched bottom. He stopped, surprised. He knew for a fact that Trickle Lake was more than 10 feet deep here. Placing his feet firmly on the ground, he stood up. And up and up. And soon he found himself standing in knee-deep water.

He looked around. Michelle and Danny were also standing up, only a few feet away, with puzzled expressions on their faces. Danny couldn't believe his eyes. They weren't standing in Trickle Lake anymore but in the center of a huge fountain in the middle of a large city center.

CHAPTER TWO

———————

Michelle's glasses had slid down her nose, and the scarf that had been tied around her head was now askew and cockeyed across her face. "What happened?" she shouted to Danny above the roar of the falling water.

Danny was dumbfounded. The three of them were standing in an enormous cement fountain. It had several tiers of water, all splashing down, one onto another, until it hit the bottom pool, where the three kids now stood. Danny looked at his feet to make sure he was where he thought he was. His feet appeared and disappeared through the white, foamy water. Coins littered the bottom and sparkled up at him. He rubbed his eyes, partly to get the water out and partly to make sure he wasn't seeing things. Everything was strange—and unusually bright.

"Get out of there!" a man shouted as he shook a cane at them. Danny looked up and took in the scene. The man had long whiskers and wore a black stovepipe hat and an open overcoat that revealed the stand-up collar on his white shirt, his black waistcoat, and black-striped trousers. He was joined by a woman with a pinched, disapproving look. She wore a frilly bonnet and a long-sleeved dress. Behind them, on a wide street, horses with riders and horse-drawn coaches moved past. Other passersby stopped to look at the three kids in the fountain.

"Where are we?" Wayne asked, his mouth hanging open in wonder.

"Didn't you hear me?" the man shouted again. "Get out of that fountain or I'll summon the constable!"

Danny started making his way to the edge of the fountain. Michelle and Wayne followed. With a lot of splashing, they got out of the fountain and sat down on the flat cement seat that circled the whole thing.

Several men and women watched them. "They weren't there a second ago," one of the women said.

"What odd clothes!" a man commented.

Danny looked down self-consciously at his wet blue jeans. "What's wrong with my clothes?" he asked indignantly.

Wayne looked offended. "You're the ones who look like you're going to a costume party," he challenged. "It's a little early for Halloween, isn't it?"

"Be quiet, Wayne," Danny said.

"Early 1800s," Michelle observed as she took off the scarf and adjusted her glasses.

"What do you mean?" Danny asked, growing more aware of the large number of people now staring at them.

"Their clothes," she replied, then waved to their surroundings. "Everything. Don't you see? It looks like the early 1800s."

Danny didn't know what she was talking about.

"Don't they teach history in your school?" she asked impatiently.

But there was no time for him to answer. A man in a smart blue uniform and blue cap pushed through the crowd. A nightstick swung from his large, black belt. "What's all this?" he inquired.

"They were swimming in the fountain," the first man said.

"We weren't swimming," Michelle corrected him. "We were *standing*."

"*I* was swimming," Wayne said helpfully. "But that was in Trickle Lake before it became this fountain."

The man in the uniform, presumably a policeman, clasped his hands behind his back and rocked back and forth on his hard, black heels. "Is that so? And why aren't you in school?" he quizzed.

"Because it's summer vacation," Michelle explained in a tone that also seemed to say, "Don't you know anything?"

"All right, come with me," the officer said and reached out to take Michelle's arm.

Michelle withdrew her arm quickly. "Where are we going?"

"That's my business," the man answered. "You just come along quietly."

"My parents taught me never to go anywhere with strangers," Michelle said as she moved away.

"Me, too," Wayne chimed in and followed her lead.

"Is that how it's going to be?" the officer asked, a threatening tone in his voice.

"I don't like this," Danny said to Michelle and Wayne.

The policeman moved toward them. "Come along with me and we'll get you sorted out." He was reaching out again and was only a step away from Michelle.

"You give me no choice," Michelle said to him. Then she shouted, "Run!"

The kids took off like sprinters who have just heard the starting pistol. Though they had no idea where they were going, they raced across an open square, then down the first street they saw. Their sneakers sploshed on the pavement as they ran across a large courtyard. A whistle blew behind them, and Danny wondered if all police officers carry whistles.

"This way!" Danny called without looking back. He ran down an alley between two large buildings. Wet footsteps echoed behind him. That alleyway led to another, which soon opened onto a major boulevard. Danny turned right and then right again down a slim pedestrian passageway. The footsteps followed, and he finally slowed down to assess who was behind him. Still going at a jog, he turned to look out of the corner of his eye. Wayne alone followed him.

"Where's Michelle?" Danny puffed.

"I thought she was right behind me," Wayne replied with a gasp.

Danny felt panicked and brushed past his brother to go back to the boulevard. Crowds of people—dressed like those they'd seen at the fountain—walked past. Horses clip-clopped and wagon wheels rattled on the road beyond. Michelle was nowhere to be seen.

"We have to go back," Danny said. Suddenly the policeman emerged from an alley and looked around for them. Danny pushed Wayne back and they retreated down the narrow passage. It doglegged to the left and then again to the right, taking them past dark doorways, dead ends, and alcoves. The buildings rose high above them, so high that the blue sky looked like a distant river in a gorge. Then, as they pressed on, the sky became obscured by disheveled wooden balconies that hung tentatively from the walls. Lines of laundry hanging out to dry crisscrossed like unraveled balls of string.

Slowing down now, Danny became aware of how trash littered the passageway and an offensive smell filled the air. Odyssey didn't have many seedy areas, but Danny recognized this as a place he didn't want to be in. The walls were scarred with wood rot and black from smoke. The boys jumped to a stop as a trash can tipped over. A scrawny cat emerged to give them an arrogant look. A woman with two dirty children disappeared into a doorway. A baby cried. A large, heavyset man appeared from another doorway, hitched up his trousers, spat on the ground, and walked in the opposite direction.

"Maybe we should go back the way we came," Danny suggested.

Wayne, who was also looking around with wide, nervous eyes, nodded. "Good idea."

As they turned to go, a thin man with wild hair and an equally wild beard stepped into their path from a nearby doorway. He was dressed in a long, tattered overcoat and smelled of cabbages. "Where are you going?" he asked with a leer. His teeth were misshapen and crooked.

Danny and Wayne glanced at one another, their feet itching to rocket them down the passageway. But the man dropped his bony hands onto their shoulders. His grip was tight.

"We're lost," Danny stammered.

"Are you?" the man asked, looking the two of them over. "That's most unfortunate."

Before they could cry out, he yanked them through the doorway and into a dark, smelly room.

Michelle hadn't been quick enough to get away from the policeman at the fountain—or the three other officers who appeared right after he blew the whistle. One held her while the others pursued Danny and Wayne. When they returned from their fruitless search, the first officer dismissed the others and, with a firm grip on her arm, took Michelle to the local police station.

"You didn't catch them, huh?" she asked as they walked down the busy street.

"No, but I'm not sure what kind of friends they are to desert you," he countered.

Michelle frowned. "They're not my friends. They're my cousins."

"For family to do such a thing to family is even worse."

In her heart, Michelle agreed. It was a rotten thing to do, leaving her behind like that. At least they could have tried to come back to rescue her. "Are you going to put me in jail?" she asked.

"I might," he replied. "But first I have to notify your parents."

"Fat chance," Michelle replied. "My father is in Seattle with his new wife, and my mother is campaigning. That's why I came to Odyssey in the first place."

The policeman glanced down at her. "Odyssey?"

"Yes."

"What's Odyssey?" he asked, his tone suspicious, as if he thought she were trying to pull a joke on him.

"It's a town," Michelle said. "*This* town."

But even as Michelle spoke the words, she knew it wasn't true. She'd visited Danny and Wayne every summer for the past four years. They had explored nearly every nook and cranny of Odyssey and most of nearby Connellsville. What she saw of this city looked nothing like either one.

At home, she had a complete, illustrated set of the works of Charles Dickens. This city reminded her of the pictures in those books. Winding streets with horse-drawn carriages; street vendors; gentlemen with top hats and ladies with broad skirts; tall, dark buildings; the spires of old churches and columns of chimneys—this city seemed to have them all. But more than anything, she was struck by how bright and color-ful everything looked, as if someone had overexposed the scene somehow. And though it made no sense to her, she asked, "Am I in London?"

"If you think you're being funny by using words I don't

know, you're wrong," the officer said. "Now keep your trap shut until we get to the station."

The police station was a plain, brick building tucked away at the end of a cul-de-sac. The policeman marched her inside and sat her down in an uncomfortable wooden chair in a large room filled with other wooden chairs and desks. "Stay here," he said firmly and disappeared through a doorway.

Blue-uniformed men came and went, sometimes with a sinister-looking man or a crying woman. Michelle watched them indifferently. Her brain was working overtime, trying to figure out where she was and how she'd gotten here. She retraced everything that had happened at Trickle Lake—the arrival of the police, the race down the dock, falling into the water—but there were no clues.

After a few minutes, the officer returned with a man who wasn't in uniform. He wore a waistcoat and trousers like many of the men in the street. He was heavyset, with a moon-shaped face and white hair pulled back in a ponytail. He said a few quick words to the policeman, who tipped a hand to his cap and left. The heavyset man approached Michelle.

"Come along, child," he said with a wave of his hand.

"Where are we going?"

"To my office, of course. We need to have a little chat."

They walked down a corridor and into a small office. The man gestured for Michelle to sit in a chair as he took a seat behind his desk. He had to move a large oil lamp to have a clear view of her.

"I'm Chief Constable Rombold," the man said. "I'm in charge here."

"I'm Michelle Brewer."

He folded his arms on the desktop and said, "I don't normally take an interest in the scamps and urchins my officers bring in, but you're an unusual case. It is my understanding that you and your cousins suddenly appeared out of thin air in the Memorial Fountain."

"I guess so."

"Can you explain how you got there?"

"No, I can't."

"Why not?"

"Because . . ." Michelle then took a deep breath and told Rombold everything that had happened up to her arrival in the fountain.

Rombold listened attentively. He betrayed no sign of whether he believed what she was saying. After she finished her explanation, he let out a long sigh. "That's quite a story," he observed.

"I know."

Rombold gazed at her for a moment. "On any other day, I might have taken you for a cheek-faced liar and thrown you in jail. But today is different." He held up a single sheet of paper that had been sitting on his desk. "We've received this communication from the palace—from Nemathes himself, in fact. Apparently, he and his wizards have determined from the alignment of the stars that something cataclysmic is about to happen to Palatia, and it will be centered in Muirk."

Michelle shook her head. "I'm sorry, but I don't know what Palatia or Muirk are. Or a Nemathes, either."

Rombold tilted his head, as if to discern whether she was telling the truth. "Muirk is the city you're now in. It is the capital city of the country of Palatia—*our* country. King Stefan is our ruler, and Nemathes is the king's supreme adviser in all matters of state."

"So I'm not in London," Michelle observed.

"No, you're not."

"Or Odyssey."

"I'm afraid not."

"Or anywhere in the United States of America or the planet earth?"

Rombold smiled as if they were playing a word game. "I've never heard of them."

"So either I'm crazy or you are."

Rombold tapped the piece of paper. "Or Nemathes is."

"Why is he crazy?" Michelle asked.

"Because he's been waiting for you."

Before Michelle had a chance to think about what he meant, there was a knock at the door. Rombold shouted for the person to enter. A man in a silver coat and breeches appeared. "Where is she?" he asked.

Rombold pointed to Michelle.

The man stepped in to get a good look at her. "I hope this isn't a wild goose chase," he said. "Nemathes won't be pleased if it is."

"If what he says is true—and what *she* says is true—he won't be disappointed," Rombold asserted, nodding to Michelle. "Good-bye, Michelle."

The man in the silver clothes guided Michelle to her feet. "Where am I going now?" she asked.

"To the palace," Rombold answered.

CHAPTER THREE

"Put your back into it!"

Danny and Wayne were on their hands and knees, scrubbing a filthy stone floor. The man who had yanked them from the alley turned out to be the owner of an inn. His name was Scurge, and the inn was called The Wilderness. Both the man and his inn were dirty and dreary.

"Slavery is against the law," Wayne complained.

Scurge booted him in the rear end hard enough to make him fall to his stomach. The bucket of brown water splashed and tipped over.

Danny leaped to his feet and faced the ugly, old codger. "Leave him alone!" he demanded.

"Shut up!" Scurge said and smacked Danny on the side of the head. It made stars dance in front of his eyes. "You two behave and you won't get hurt. I need a little help, that's all. My normal boys ran off. I've got to have the place cleaned up for the customers tonight. I'm even willing to pay you, if you're nicelike. But if you're gonna complain, I'll tie you up and throw you in the cellar for the rats to nibble on."

Danny and Wayne exchanged glances, refilled the bucket, and went back to work.

"That's better," Scurge said as he turned to leave. "And don't forget to scrub under those tables and chairs." Then he stopped and added, "Don't get any ideas about escaping, either. The doors and shutters are all locked tight."

After Scurge left, Wayne leaned to Danny and whispered, "What's going on here?"

"I don't know," Danny replied. "Everything has happened so fast that I haven't had time to think."

"I was hoping maybe this whole thing was a dream until he kicked me," Wayne said. "But I *felt* that," he added, rubbing his backside.

Danny shook his head. "It's not a dream. Somehow when we fell into Trickle Lake, we wound up here." He looked around at the scarred wood that made up the beams, counter, chairs, and tables. "We're definitely not in Odyssey anymore."

"Just like the Wizard of Oz! We're having a fairy tale adventure!"

"It's not an adventure!" Danny snapped. "This is serious."

The two boys scrubbed for another few minutes.

"But how do we get back home?" Wayne eventually asked.

Danny looked around for Scurge, then said, "I think our first problem is getting out of this dump."

Wayne leaned back to face his brother. "I say we knock him out with the bucket and run for it."

"And if it doesn't work, we're done for," Danny countered, then looked fully at his brother. Something was different about him, but at first he didn't know what. Then he realized what had changed. Wayne's eyes, which had always been dark gray, were now different colors. "What happened to your eyes?" Danny asked.

Wayne's mouth fell open with surprise. "What happened to *your* eyes?" he said in amazement.

"Yours have changed colors. One is blue, and the other is green."

"The same with yours!" Wayne exclaimed.

Danny touched his eyes. "Really?" He thought about it for a moment. "I wonder if there was something in the fountain water that did it, like chlorine or something. Have you noticed how bright all the colors are?"

"Yeah," Wayne said. "I thought it was just me."

Scurge suddenly appeared in the doorway. "Quit your jabbering and get back to work!" he shouted.

The boys worked hard all afternoon, scrubbing the floors, the tables, and the chairs. Then Scurge had them clean all the dishes and help him roll out the barrels of drinks for the customers that night. Next, just after they'd lit all the lamps and candles and he was about to open the doors for business, Scurge grabbed Wayne and threw him into the cellar. He locked the door with a large key.

"Why'd you do that?" Danny asked as Wayne pounded on the door.

"Because I need you to serve tonight. I won't have to worry about you running out the door with him locked up in there, if you know what I mean."

Wayne kept pounding on the door until Danny told him to stop. "Just take it easy!" Danny called to him.

"But it's dark in here," Wayne complained. "And I think I hear things moving around."

"I'll figure something out," Danny assured him. But he felt ill because he had no idea how to get them out of this predicament.

Scurge opened the inn's doors and shutters. A handful of men entered, all of them looking as if they'd crawled out from under the same rock as Scurge. They could have been pirates from *Treasure Island* or ruffians from *Oliver Twist*. Whoever they were, Danny's heart sank at the sight of them. They wouldn't help him or his brother even if he begged for it.

Soon the inn was packed with customers, and Danny ran

himself ragged keeping up with their demands. He had to juggle trays of drinks and the greenish selection of cold meats Scurge put on offer. If Danny made a mistake or accidentally spilled anything, someone smacked him on the head or gave him a hard kick. He started to feel like a giant bruise.

Later, he went to the cellar door and knocked. "Are you all right?" he asked his brother.

"Just sitting here," Wayne replied.

"You're not afraid, are you?"

"Not anymore."

Danny was surprised. "Why not?"

"I've been praying for help," Wayne replied.

Scurge rounded the corner just then and glared at Danny. "What are you doing?" he demanded.

"I was checking on my brother."

Scurge caught hold of Danny's shirt and started dragging him back to the customers. Danny tried to get away, but Scurge kept up with him, slapping him until they were in the main dining room.

"Help!" Danny cried out.

No one even looked up.

"You see?" Scurge hissed. "Nobody cares."

Suddenly, a tall, imposing man stood in front of them. He was dressed in a buckskin coat and trousers, rough-sewn leather boots, and a coonskin cap. He had a rugged face and bushy beard and mustache. He carried a large satchel and a long walking stick, which he rapped on the counter.

Scurge looked up at the man nervously, then gave Danny a shove. "Go on. Get back to work," he ordered.

The tall man put a restraining hand on Danny's shoulder. "Wait," he said in a low voice. He glared at Scurge. "In my day, you wouldn't get away with this kind of abuse."

Scurge was scared but defiant. "It's none of your business," he insisted.

"Seeing you beat this boy makes it my business," the man said. He looked down at Danny, and they made eye contact. Danny gasped. This man had different-colored eyes, too, one blue and the other green! A flicker of surprise crossed the man's face as he noticed the same about Danny's eyes. "You don't belong here, do you?" he asked Danny.

"No, sir."

Scurge sneered at the man. "Are you going to drink or not? The boy has work to do!"

Quick as lightning, the man grabbed Scurge by the lapels. "This boy doesn't belong here," he said softly but with a clearly threatening tone.

"Let go of me!" Scurge squirmed, trying to free himself from the man's grasp. The room went quiet.

"I'm leaving now and taking this boy with me," the big man declared.

"My brother," Danny said. "He's got my brother locked in the cellar."

"You can't!" Scurge whined. "These boys work for me!"

A man from another table stood up. He had a patch over one eye. "What's this all about?" he challenged.

The man glared at him silently.

The one-eyed man hesitated, sized up his opponent, then sat down again. "Never mind," he said.

The man shook Scurge. "Keys, please," he demanded.

Scurge fumbled in his pockets and pulled out a key. "It's this one."

"Let your brother out," the man told Danny.

Danny snatched the key from Scurge and raced back to free his brother.

"What's happening?" Wayne asked as he stepped into the hallway and rubbed his eyes.

"We're getting out of here."

"Far out! I'm glad I was praying."

When Danny and Wayne returned to the front room, the man let go of Scurge. "Your day is ending," the man said. "A new day is coming. You have my word."

"So *you* say," Scurge growled. "I don't know who you think you are, coming in here like this."

The man picked up an old apple from the counter and pushed his fist against it. Only then did Danny notice that he had a large ring on his forefinger. The man tossed the apple to Scurge, who looked at it closely.

Scurge went bug-eyed. "The royal seal? Your ring bears the royal seal?" Scurge swallowed hard and searched the man's face. His face fell with recognition. "Can it be? *Prince Fendar?*"

The change in the room was immediate. All heads turned toward them in a stunned silence.

The man gestured for Danny and Wayne to head for the door. "Let's go," he instructed quietly.

"You've come back?" Scurge called after them. "You *dared* to come back? The king's men will kill you if they find you! I'll tell them and collect the reward myself!"

Danny and Wayne stepped outside. Scurge was still shouting as the man also crossed the room. He kept an eye on the customers, then closed the door to the inn behind him. Night had fallen, and thick clouds obscured the sky. The city street was deserted. Dim lights from candles and lamps dotted the doorways and windows, splashing a dull, yellow glow on the cobblestone streets.

"Are you really a prince who's wanted by the police?" Wayne asked, impressed.

"Yes."

"Where are we supposed to go now?" Danny interrupted.

"I'm supposed to meet someone here, so let's stay close." The man gestured to the dark entrance to an alley. "We'll wait there."

When they were safe in the shadows, Danny thanked the man for helping them.

"You're welcome," the man said. "Now, what are your names?"

The two boys introduced themselves.

The man bowed slightly. "As you already heard, I am Fendar." He then stepped aside to allow some of the light from the street lamp to shine on their faces.

"Both of you are voices," the man said, a hint of awe in his tone.

Danny was confused. "Are what?"

Fendar tugged at his beard thoughtfully. "We haven't had a child sent to us as a voice since . . . since the days of Connam. And now we have *two*. What are you doing here?"

"We don't know," Danny replied.

"Did you come from Marus?" Fendar asked.

"We came from Odyssey," Wayne chimed in.

"Where is Odyssey?"

"Near Connellsville," Wayne answered.

Somehow Danny knew the names wouldn't mean anything to Fendar. "I guess you could say that we're lost," he admitted.

Fendar pondered this for a moment. "There are only two of you?"

"Michelle, our cousin, is around somewhere, too."

"We lost her when they chased us from the fountain," added Wayne.

The man looked at the two boys as if he understood something that Danny hadn't figured out yet. Danny wished he would explain it to him, but just then the sound of footsteps came echoing up the cobbled street. A minute later, a man as large as Fendar approached The Wilderness Inn, and Fendar stepped out to intercept him. "Wondrar!" he whispered.

The man swung around to Fendar, then rushed across the street. The two men clasped each other in a warm and robust embrace. By the street lamp, Danny could see that the other man looked like a slightly older version of Fendar, but he had a trimmer beard and was dressed in the fashion they'd seen all day. Danny thought again of how Michelle had said that the styles were like those from the 1800s.

Wondrar held Fendar at arm's length, his eyes misty with tears. "I had a dream that you'd come back to Muirk—that you were here in this very spot," Wondrar said. "I hardly dared believe it. But I had to find out for myself, so I rushed out of bed to come here." He laughed and waved a hand at his shirt. "This is my bed shirt!"

"The dream was from the Unseen One," Fendar explained. "It was the only way to tell you to meet me."

"It's a good thing I take my dreams seriously," Wondrar said, then suddenly hugged his brother again. "And I thank Him that He brought you back safe and sound."

Fendar laughed. "For such a formidable older brother, you always were a soft touch."

Wondrar dabbed his eyes. "Look at you! The forests of Gotthard have turned you into a wildebeest."

"Am I not fashionable?" Fendar asked, taking feigned offense.

"Only to another wildebeest," Wondrar answered with a laugh. He then turned his attention to Danny and Wayne. "Are these your children?"

"No, no," Fendar responded. "I've just met them. But I believe they're important to why I've come. Look closely at their eyes."

Wondrar did. "Ah!"

"And there is a third child. I'll wager my boots that she's a voice as well," said Fendar.

"I see."

"But *I* don't," Danny said impatiently. "What's going on here?"

"I'll explain as much as I can later," Fendar said. "Where is it safe to go?" he asked Wondrar.

"A friend of mine is a tradesman who travels abroad for a wealthy Palatian. He has an apartment on the edge of the Marutian district that you can use."

"The Marutian *district?*"

"Yes, we've all been herded into our own part of the city. We have our own shops, our own commerce, a governing council—everything we could possibly want. We come out only to work."

"Is it a ghetto?" Fendar asked.

"No. On the contrary, it is comfortable and well-cared-for by the king and his governors."

Fendar looked unhappy. "How shrewd. No wonder the desire to return to Marus has all but vanished."

Wondrar agreed. "Under these conditions, few Marutians think of themselves as slaves. One or two small rebel groups try to keep the flame of freedom alight, but most of the people don't want to hear about it. They don't want to ruin a good situation."

"I will want to meet with the rebels," Fendar stated. "I will want to meet with *all* the leaders of our people. A change is coming. The Unseen One has promised it."

"Still, meeting with our leaders is a dangerous idea. There are spies everywhere. The king will know you've returned."

Fendar gestured to The Wilderness Inn. "I've already announced my arrival. I have no doubt that someone is on the way to tell the king even now."

"He'll kill you."

"Let him try."

Bewildered and tired, Danny walked with Wayne a few steps behind Fendar and Wondrar. The two men chatted on and on about people and places Danny had never heard of. He wished someone would stop long enough to tell him what was going on. Keeping mostly to the smaller streets and alleyways to avoid the police, they eventually came to a part of the city with buildings that looked like a new apartment complex. This was the Marutian district of Muirk. The entire area was enclosed by a high wall. A single large gate was the only way in or out.

"Everyone calls it 'The Promised Land,'" Wondrar explained as they passed through the gate. "Some say so facetiously, while others mean it sincerely." Wondrar led them to a brownstone building and up a flight of stairs to a door. He felt along the upper edge of the doorjamb and found the key that would let them in. Wondrar stepped in first and began to light a lamp and then various candles.

The apartment was small and cozy. It had a main living area with chairs and a sofa, a dining table, and a kitchenette. A small hallway led to two bedrooms beyond. Once they were settled in, Wondrar announced he would leave right away to talk to the Marutian elders and the rebel leaders. "You should be safe here until I come back," he said and left.

"I'm so confused," Danny told Fendar. "Will you *please* tell us what's happening?"

"Tell me your story and we'll try to figure it out together," said Fendar.

Danny, with occasional interjections from Wayne, explained to Fendar everything that had happened to them.

"So you are from another world," Fendar concluded.

"We are?" Wayne asked, amazed. "We're like creatures from another planet?"

"In a sense, you must be."

Danny eyed Fendar skeptically. "You don't seem very surprised," he said.

"This isn't the first time the Unseen One has brought children to us from another world."

"What is an Unseen One?" Wayne asked.

"Not *what* but *who*," Fendar explained. "The Unseen One is the Supreme Creator, the God of all gods, the true King and Master of all."

"Oh! We have one of those in our world," Wayne said enthusiastically. "But we call Him God."

"Then He is the same as the Unseen One. The Lord is One."

"But what are we doing here?" Danny asked. "Why did He bring us here?"

"According to our Sacred Scrolls, the Unseen One promised to bring about our freedom through three children. The Sacred Scrolls say:

'By the word of a child, the signs will begin.

By the word of a child, the heart will deny.

By the word of a child, the clouds will rise.'"

"But what does that mean?" Danny asked.

"I assume we'll find out in time." Fendar suddenly frowned. "What did you say became of your cousin?"

"We don't know," Danny answered.

"I'll bet she was caught by the police," said Wayne. "She was never a very fast runner."

"In that case, the king probably knows you're here."

"So?"

"That means the whole palace is probably worried."

"About *us?*" asked Danny, surprised. "But why?"

"The Palatians have their own beliefs, including books and sayings that involve a lot of wizardry and nonsense like that. But sometimes, rarely, they get part of the story right. According to their Ancient Oracles, they know that three children are to come whose arrival will signal the rise of a new power. They believe it is a power that may one day destroy all of Palatia. So, naturally, they're afraid of it."

Danny shook his head. It was all too much to believe. "But we're just some kids from Odyssey! We can't be the three children you're talking about."

Fendar smiled through his thick beard. "We'll see about that."

Without meaning to, Wayne yawned.

Fendar stood up. "It's late. You both need some sleep."

"But you promised to tell us your story," Wayne argued.

"I will—*after* you get some rest." He ushered them into one of the bedrooms. It had only one bed, but the bed was large, and the two boys could stretch out without bumping into each other.

The last thing Danny wondered as he drifted to sleep was how he fit into this whole adventure. Were he and Wayne and Michelle really part of some ancient prophecy? And if they were, what were they expected to do?

CHAPTER FOUR

◆————————◆

Michelle opened her eyes and looked around. Everything was a sleepy blur, but she knew right away that she wasn't in her bed at Danny and Wayne's house. She sat up quickly and tried to rub the sleep from her eyes. She was in a large bed with a canopy. Thick curtains hung on tall windows. Tapestries decorated the walls, most of them with crests of a giant eagle standing in the middle of a garland. A huge fireplace adorned the far wall, red embers dying in the grate. Her clothes and sneakers were on a rack next to it. Deep brown paneling covered the rest. It was luxurious. It was like being in a palace.

The palace, she suddenly remembered.

The king's guard had taken her to the palace known by all as Muirkostle. It had ornate front gates and a long expanse of lawn and a driveway leading to the front door. Made of gray stone, with towers and turrets springing up from different sections, it seemed to Michelle to be a fairy-tale castle.

She had been ushered by the guard through two enormous double doors and then led down a series of dark halls to a room. It looked like some sort of study, with three walls covered with fully stocked bookshelves and the fourth wall taken up by a fireplace. It had yawned blackly at her as she sat down in a velvet-covered chair. Above the fireplace had been a crest with a giant eagle standing in the center of a garland.

The guard had left her. As she waited, her eye had caught a piece of paper on a nearby table. The paper looked like the one Rombold had waved around. She had glanced at the door, then stepped over to the table.

"Be on the Lookout!" large, black letters had shouted from the page. Underneath, in smaller, crudely printed type, it had said, "An announcement from His Majesty's adviser." After that had been a paragraph that said:

> The King's seers have determined from the
> configurations of the stars and the signs of
> the Ancient Oracles that we are on the
> threshold of great concerns. Be on the look-
> out for three children of unusual speech,
> manners, attributes, or clothing. If you
> encounter any three children or a single child
> who fits this description, dispatch an urgent
> notification to Nemathes at Muirkostle.

Michelle had read the page three times before it suddenly dawned on her what it meant. "They think I'm one of the three children!" she had said to herself.

"Aren't you?" a deep voice had asked from the other side of the room.

It seemed like a dream to her now, but at the time Michelle had cried out and nearly knocked over the small table. She had looked at the door, sure someone had come in without her hearing, but no one was there.

"Well?" the voice had asked again, and Michelle had looked over by the fireplace. The man had stood with his arm resting on the mantelpiece, as if he'd been there for some time. Michelle had wondered how he had gotten into the room.

Confused, Michelle had answered, "There were three of us. But I don't know anything about stars and signs."

The man was completely bald and had a slender, waxen face. Michelle hadn't been able to guess his age. He had been dressed in a robe of deep red that was open at the front. Beneath that he'd worn a black shirt and trousers, in the style of the kinds of clothes she'd seen already.

"There are 12 signs from the Ancient Oracles," the man had said, his voice seeming to shake the rafters. "These signs are to be the mark of the rise of a great country to the north, a great people from whom will come the Great Message from the Leader who will one day rule the world. One of the signs is the appearance of three mysterious children who claim to come from another world and who will do wonders to help give birth to the new nation. Naturally, I was concerned to hear about three children who suddenly appeared in the Memorial Fountain."

"I don't know how we got into the fountain."

The man had then eyed her from head to foot, which had given Michelle the creeps. "You are dressed rather strangely. And according to the chief constable, you claim to be from places we've never heard of. Perhaps you've come from another world?"

"I don't know about that," Michelle had said. "But if I'm supposed to do some kind of wonders, nobody told *me* about it."

"Where are your friends?"

"My *cousins* ran off. I don't know where they are."

"They left you to fend for yourself? All alone in this big city?" The man had moved toward her, his hands clasped in front of him. "How rude."

"What do you expect? They're boys."

"We'll have to find them for you. It wouldn't be to anyone's advantage if anything bad happened to them."

"Serves them right for leaving me behind," Michelle had said.

The man had suddenly looked closely at Michelle's eyes.

It had made her nervous, and she had instinctively stepped back from him.

"Ah, I see," the man had said.

"See what?"

The man had ignored her question and said in a voice as thick as his velvet robe, "The king would be upset if anyone thought he were less than a genial host to . . . a special *foreigner*. You will stay here at the palace as our guest. Whatever you want, we will provide."

"I'd like to let my sneakers dry. They're still wet."

"Of course," the man had said. "My name is Nemathes, by the way."

And so Nemathes had brought Michelle to this room. He had arranged to have something brought for her to wear while her own clothes dried next to the fire. He had also had a servant, a woman named Morgon, stay at her beck and call for the rest of the day. She had eaten two wonderful meals of food she couldn't identify but certainly enjoyed. Morgon had also accompanied her for walks around the grounds and gardens of the palace. The colors of the summer day had dazzled her. The grass was the greenest she'd ever seen. The reds, purples, and yellows of the flowers were incredibly vibrant. *It's amazing,* she had thought.

Morgon wasn't very talkative and hadn't readily answered any of Michelle's questions. Finally she had gotten Morgon to tell her a little about where they were and a brief history of Palatia's rise as one of the greatest powers in the world. Muirk was its showpiece, the crowning glory of all that Palatia's kings had achieved over the past few hundred years. King Stefan, Morgon had said, was the greatest of all the kings.

That night, Michelle had gone to bed with her head

swimming with the wonder of Palatia. Though she'd still had no better idea about why she was there than when she'd first stepped out of the fountain, she had realized things could be worse. At least she was comfortable and the guest of the king himself. Sort of.

Once or twice she had thought about Danny and Wayne and wondered where they were. She had secretly hoped they were miserable. *That'll teach them for running off without me,* she had thought.

Michelle's thoughts were brought back into the present as Morgon came into the room with a tray of food. It was a full breakfast of eggs, toast, something that tasted like bacon, baked beans, mushrooms, and tomatoes. While Michelle ate, Morgon left and returned with clothes for Michelle to wear that day.

"What's wrong with my own clothes?" Michelle asked. "They should be dry by now."

"Your clothes aren't appropriate—not for today," Morgon answered, laying out a silk dress of purples and light blues.

"What's so special about today?" Michelle asked as she admired the dress.

"You're going to meet the king."

Michelle's heart leaped. She was going to meet a king!

Morgon helped her to dress, then opened a door to a wardrobe that had a large mirror inside. Michelle stepped up to it to brush her hair. It was the first time she'd looked at herself since she'd arrived in Palatia.

She gasped and stepped back, dropping the brush and putting a hand to her mouth.

"What's wrong?" Morgon asked.

"My eyes!"

"What about them?"

Michelle took off her glasses and looked more closely at her reflection. "They're different colors!"

Fendar woke Danny and Wayne the next morning. He startled them at first because he had shaved off his beard and mustache. He was still a ruggedly handsome man, with sun-baked cheeks and dancing eyes, but now they could see the square and determined jaw that made him look truly princelike. He'd also gotten rid of his wilderness outfit and put on a white shirt, black coat, black trousers, and black boots. Danny guessed him to be about 50 years old.

Danny and Wayne had a dozen questions they wanted to ask Fendar, like how he was a prince but was wanted by the police, why he'd been away from Palatia for so long, and what were the forests of Gotthard that Wondrar had mentioned. But they didn't get a chance, as Wondrar arrived shortly after they sat down to a simple breakfast of eggs and toast.

"I've arranged a meeting first thing this morning," he said. "I have to warn you, most of the elders weren't pleased to hear of your return. They think it's a portent of trouble."

Fendar sighed. "Are they so blinded by the comforts and security of Palatia that they've forgotten who they are—and where they belong?" he asked.

Wondrar didn't reply.

"Hopefully their eyes will be opened by what I have to say."

"What *are* you going to say?" Wondrar asked. "You haven't told me much, you know."

"I will tell everything there is to tell at the gathering of the elders," Fendar promised, putting his hand on his brother's arm. "But you are vital to the Unseen One's plans."

"I'm happy to be of service," Wondrar replied.

Once they had eaten their breakfast, Wondrar insisted that they make their way to the gathering of the elders. The Promised Land by day was a beehive of activity. The Marutians all wore nearly identical clothes—the dull-gray uniforms of servants. Wondrar explained as they walked that the Marutians would spread out over the city to take their positions as household servants, factory workers, or office clerks. Others would go out to the fields to work the livestock or crops. They weren't paid directly for their work but were given vouchers that could be used in the shops and service centers of the Marutian district.

In a sense, the Marutians were given nearly everything they could reasonably expect in exchange for their hard work. But they weren't allowed to leave the city without permission, nor could they ever rise to become anything more than servants. King Stefan maintained a firm but seemingly benevolent control over his slaves. Occasionally a policeman strolled through the area.

They entered a one-story building that served as a community hall for the district. Several men were already waiting as Fendar and Wondrar went to the front. Danny and Wayne sat down in a couple of chairs off to the side. The men watched them suspiciously. No one spoke to either Fendar or Wondrar until a few stragglers arrived, took their seats, and the doors were closed.

A man with thin, silver hair stood up and addressed himself to Fendar. "As Wondrar and the rest of our colleagues already know, I am Regmund, the chief elder of this assembly," he began. "I was a friend of your father's while he was still alive, may the Unseen One keep him in peace. I believe you know most of the men here." To this Fendar nodded. Reg-mund continued, "So tell us what this is all about. You must know the great risk we are taking by meeting with you, a fugi-tive."

"As I have risked much by coming back to you," Fendar said seriously. "But the Unseen One has sent me, and I must obey Him." Fendar scanned the crowd and said with a hint of accusation, "I assume we Marutians still believe in the Unseen One."

Another older man with deep wrinkles and white hair pounded his hand on the chair in front of him. "Don't take a self-righteous tone with us, young man," he snapped. "While you were being wet-nursed and coddled in Muirkostle, I, Elder Langton, and the rest of us were down here, worshiping the Unseen One you now claim to serve."

A couple of the men said, "Here! Here!"

"You speak true, Elder Langton," Fendar said calmly. "But you'll remember that it was not my choice to go to Muirkostle. I was taken there as a baby and nurtured as a member of the royal family by King Akaron and Queen Leviatha. They raised me as their own child, alongside Stefan, who is now the king. But surely you have heard the story."

"Not from *your* lips," another elder said.

"Then let me speak openly. I was raised as a Palatian with-out knowing I was a Marutian. No one told me of Marus, that great country to the north. In my sheltered upbringing, I had come to believe it was a barren wilderness, inhabited by noth-ing but wild animals. How could I know of its former great-ness, or of how our ancestors came to Palatia during the Great Famines in the time of Connam?"

So he was a slave boy who was adopted by the king and raised to be a prince, Danny thought. *That's not such a bad deal.*

"But on the day as a young man when I found through a servant that I was really a Marutian, I took the news to heart. In secret, I sought out my family and finally met my older brother, Wondrar, and my sisters and my parents. Also in secret, I studied the history and traditions of my people. And, as you well know, this put me in disfavor with the king when he found out—especially when I affirmed my belief in the Unseen One."

The group of elders listened in silence.

Fendar continued, "The king and his family tried to force me to stay away from you, the Marutians. But I couldn't. My heart burned for you. I saw what the king was doing to you— killing your spirit and your will to be free through the bribery of comfort and security—and it brought tears to my eyes day in and day out. I yearned to be with you, body and soul."

Pausing for a moment, Fendar lowered his head as if the memory of what he was about to say was a heavy weight on him. "Then came the day when I learned of the king's plot to drive my family out of Palatia by force. The king mistakenly thought that if I could not see my family again, I would forget my lineage and heritage. But my true father, a man of indomitable spirit, refused to leave Muirk without me. He defied the king's soldiers, who then began to beat him terribly. I witnessed this and intervened. In the struggle, I accidentally killed one of the soldiers."

"So *that's* why he's a wanted man," Wayne whispered.

"My fate was sealed. I knew I couldn't help my family or any of the other Marutians while I was considered a murderer, so I escaped west to the forests of Gotthard. There I made a living for myself, married, and have hidden away all these years—until the Unseen One told me to come back."

"He *spoke* to you?" Regmund asked.

"Yes, He did."

"You will have to be more specific than that," one of the elders said.

"I will. He spoke to me from the mouth of a baby lamb."

The elders muttered among themselves. A couple of them laughed.

"I was walking through the forest one day and came upon a pasture. In the middle stood a single lamb. I thought the lamb had somehow been separated from a flock, but then He *spoke* to me." He paused to let his statement sink in. "'Child,' He said. He spoke to me as clearly as I am speaking to you now. I fell to my knees and hid my face, because I *knew* in my heart that this was the Unseen One. But I dared to ask the lamb for proof.

"'Behold,' the lamb said to me. Suddenly, a chalice appeared on a nearby rock. I hadn't noticed it before, and I would have had it been there when I first walked up. The chalice began to glow, as if from a bright lamp inside.

"'Drink from the chalice,' the lamb said. 'Drink until it is empty.'

"My fingers trembled as I took the chalice and drank from it. It was the purest water I had ever tasted. To this day, I feel refreshed in my very soul to think about it.

"Then the lamb said, 'There was a time when the Marutians called to Me for deliverance from their slavery, but now they have become as the Palatians. I heard their cries, and now I hear their silence. The time has come for all Marutians to return to their true home in Marus.' Even as I marveled at those words, the lamb commanded me to bear the responsibility for the journey home. 'You will lead them out,' He said."

The elders now openly scoffed. "We've heard enough!" one shouted.

Fendar held up his hands for silence. "I couldn't believe it, either," he continued after they had calmed down. "I told the lamb it was not possible. As a prince of Palatia, I felt like an outcast from my own Marutian people. I was also a murderer and an outcast from Palatia. If I tried to lead, who would follow?

"But the Unseen One was firm in His call upon me and said He would empower Wondrar to be my helper. He commanded me to leave my wife and children and return to Muirk immediately. And then a most wondrous and mysterious thing happened."

Fendar paused to survey the room. He swallowed hard, as if he knew this would be the most difficult thing to explain. "Suddenly, the lamb began to bleed from wounds that appeared in His feet and His side. I didn't understand it at all and rushed forward to help. But He commanded me to stop. He said, 'My innocent blood has been shed for you in ways you cannot know, but they will be revealed at the right time. Collect my blood in the chalice, and carry it to Palatia. You will need it there.' So I picked up the chalice and held it close to the lamb's feet and side. Then I covered it and have carried it with me in my satchel." Fendar waved toward his satchel, which he had hung from a hook on the wall.

Danny and Wayne looked at each other. It all sounded strangely familiar to them from church and yet, in ways, unlike anything they'd ever heard before.

"I have obeyed the Unseen One, and I am here to lead the people of Marus out of Palatia," Fendar concluded in a firm voice. "We are not meant for this land but for another—our true home."

Regmund stood up. "Thank you for telling us your story, Fendar," he said coldly, "but I think I speak for all present

when I say that your words, while inspiring, are also imprac-
tical. First, you will have a hard time convincing most of our
citizens that it would be in their best interests to leave their
lives and homes here to go to an untamed wilderness. Yes, it
was the home of our ancestors, but is it ours? This we do not
know."

"The Unseen One made a promise to Marus himself about
the future of our nation," Fendar countered. "We are to be a
light to the world, the messengers of a great truth. But we are
neither as long as we are the *slaves* of Palatia."

"Slaves?" one of the elders cried out. "You dare to call us
slaves? Is that how this new generation of upstarts refers to
hard work and industry? We came to this land as strangers,
and we have become accepted."

"Yes," Fendar said with a nod. "Accepted as *slaves*. Don't
be fooled by the so-called generosity of the king. Remember, I
lived in the palace for years. I heard their plans. They decided
to lull you into peace, to dull your hearts to messages of freedom by giving you houses that are not your homes and food
you cannot claim as your own. They have seduced you to
sleep, and even now you slumber."

The elders were indignant at this. Some stood up as if they
might walk out.

A young man with curly, brown hair and a thin beard stood
and shouted at them to calm down. "Listen, brothers!" he cried
out. "Don't be too quick to reject what Prince Fendar—"

"Fendar, please," Fendar corrected him. "I do not accept
the title."

"I am Jakin," the young man went on. "I am a leader of a
small group who believe as you do."

"I knew it wouldn't be long before you'd speak up," an
elder complained.

"You can count on us to help in any way we can," Jakin told Fendar, who looked at him gratefully.

Langton banged his chair against the floor. "This is all ideal-istic nonsense!" he complained. "Even if we wanted to go, King Stefan would not let us. Why would he sit back and let his best working population leave?"

"That's right," agreed Regmund. "How will you convince the king to let us go? You haven't the power to do it."

Without answering, Fendar walked over to Wondrar. "My walking stick," he said. It was leaning against the wall, and Wondrar handed it over. Fender walked to where Regmund stood and held the stick close to him. Before everyone's very eyes, it transformed into a sword. Everyone took a step back except Regmund, who seemed glued to his chair. Danny and Wayne were on their feet now. With both hands, Fendar lifted the sword point down and drove it into the floor. He let go and stood back.

"What is this?" Regmund asked anxiously.

The handle of the sword suddenly moved and shook as thin, vinelike branches shot out from it. Then from the branches sprouted leaves until a miniature tree stood in the center of the hall.

Fendar said, "If we put our faith in the Unseen One, our nation will flourish like a tree beside a deep river."

Regmund was clearly astounded but still unyielding. "Magic tricks?" he asked. "You're going to convince King Stefan by performing magic tricks?"

No sooner had he said those words than the branches reached out for him like a hundred spindly fingers. They wrapped around him and drew him close for a terrible embrace. Before he could lift his arms to fend them off, they had him circled and covered. In a matter of a minute, he was wrapped in a cocoon of wood and green. From inside, they could hear him gasping for air.

Langton and the rest of the elders begged Fendar to free Regmund. "He'll suffocate in there!" one said.

"Have mercy," Langton pleaded.

Fendar stooped down and grabbed the bottom of the tree. It quickly withdrew its branches from Regmund, leaving him to collapse to the ground, struggling for breath. In the twinkling of an eye, the tree had disappeared completely and Fendar once again stood with a walking stick in his hand.

"Far out!" Wayne said softly.

Fendar gazed coolly at the gasping Regmund and told him, "It's a mistake to *ever* call the works of the Unseen One *magic*."

The elders now looked at Fendar with more respect, if not outright fear, and waited to hear what he would say next. But Fendar didn't speak. He retrieved his satchel from the wall and headed for the door.

"Wait!" Jakin called. "What are you going to do?"

"We are going to meet the king," Fendar replied. He waved a hand toward Wondrar, Danny, and Wayne and said, "Come on."

Danny and Wayne both pointed to themselves and asked, "Who, *us*?"

CHAPTER FIVE

Michelle went through all the possible reasons her eyes might have changed colors, but to no avail. She'd never heard of eyes changing colors in someone her age. Ever.

Nemathes arrived to escort her to the king. He approved of her outfit and said she looked lovely. Then they walked together down various halls to the king.

As they went, Michelle asked hesitantly, "Do you notice anything strange about my eyes?"

Nemathes gazed at her eyes and nodded. "They are beautiful," he replied.

"But they're different colors," Michelle said. "And I don't know why. My eyes were hazel before."

Nemathes stopped at a large, gold-framed door. He faced her and explained, "There are legends of children with powers—remarkable powers—who had eyes like yours. Perhaps you are one of those children." He opened the door, then whispered, "I believe you are."

They stepped into the room to meet the king.

Michelle liked King Stefan right away. He was tall and good-looking, with a strong physique and piercing eyes. A ringlet of gold rested on his sandy-colored hair like a fallen halo. He had a trim beard and mustache that framed his full lips and made his smile larger and brighter than it might have been without them. Michelle figured he must be in his late 30s or early 40s.

They met in his reception room, where he was consulting with his advisers. He stopped everything when Nemathes brought Michelle in. He rose from his throne, took her hand, and kissed the back of it.

"This is, indeed, an honor," he said.

For the first time in years, Michelle actually giggled. She blushed and then remembered what Nemathes had told her to do. She took up the folds of her dress and curtsied. "Thank you, Your Highness," she responded.

The king signaled, and his advisers left the room. Only Nemathes remained. A servant brought a chair over and placed it near the throne. Above the throne was the now-familiar crest of the eagle and garland. "I want to hear all about your adventures," the king encouraged. "Nemathes has told me some of it, but I think it would be better coming from your lips."

Michelle adjusted her glasses and told the king everything that had happened to her. She concluded by saying, "Sometimes I think I'm in a wild dream. I don't know how I got here, and I'm not even sure any of this is real."

King Stefan had been listening attentively, with his face resting against his hand. He lifted his head and looked playfully affronted. "You wouldn't relegate us to the land of dreams, would you?" he asked. "Not so soon after we met. What if you were to wake up right now? Then I wouldn't have a chance to get to know you better."

Michelle giggled again.

"But there's this other business to think about," the king continued. "According to Nemathes, whom I trust with my life, your appearance here is part of an ancient prophecy. What do you know about that?"

"I've never heard of it before, Your Highness," Michelle answered.

"You came with two boys, you said."

"That's true. But they don't know anything about it, either. We just showed up, that's all."

The king looked thoughtfully at Nemathes, then said to Michelle, "You're too charming to be a threat to me. So I can only assume you are here to do me good somehow. Legends speak of children being wiser than men. And I know of other legends about children from other worlds affecting the fate of nations. Perhaps you have been sent from your world to advise me, to lead me into this new age Nemathes keeps talking about."

Michelle smiled. "I'll help if I can."

"Good!" the king said as he slapped his hands on the armrests of the throne. "Then our first order of business is for you to stay at my side. I want you to witness what happens here in the palace and tell me what you think."

Michelle gasped. "You want to know what *I* think?"

Nemathes cleared his throat. "Majesty, is that wise?" he asked. "She is a *girl* after all. Many of your advisers and council members might take exception to having a *girl* attend your meetings."

"What does her being a girl have anything to do with it?" King Stefan retorted sharply. "As my chief adviser, I would expect you not to be so narrow-minded. If the great powers that rule our world have sent me a girl to be my helper, who am I to reject her?"

Nemathes bowed stiffly at the rebuke.

King Stefan winked at Michelle. And Michelle knew then that she liked the king *a lot*.

◆————————◆

Throughout the morning, the king made sure to introduce Michelle to all his advisers and councillors. She liked being treated special. And even though some of them gave her wary glances, she was resolved to stay true to her job. She would listen carefully and advise the king when he asked.

Unfortunately for her, most of the meetings were about things she barely understood. They talked about farming output, industrial productivity, economic imports, fiscal yields, budgets, labor problems, and so on. She found her brain getting thick with boredom.

Then something happened to cause a stir. A messenger arrived late in the morning, went straight to the throne, and whispered in the king's ear. King Stefan's face registered the news. He cheeks burned, and he leaped to his feet and shouted, "He's here in Muirk? And he dares to come here to the *palace*? Is he insane?"

Nemathes was the only one who had the courage to speak. "To whom do you refer, Majesty?" he asked.

"Fendar, who else?" he roared. Michelle and everyone else squirmed in their seats as Stefan began to pace. Then he suddenly pointed an accusing finger at Nemathes. "And don't tell me you didn't know about this, Nemathes. You know everything that goes on in this country. A cockroach doesn't sneeze in the Caves of Laurel without you hearing about it."

Nemathes bowed, as if to concede to the statement. "I had heard Prince Fendar had returned—"

"Don't call him *Prince!* No one is ever to call him that! He was an illegitimate child who betrayed my father and my entire family." King Stefan fumed. "I'm glad my parents are not alive to see this day."

"What is your pleasure, Your Majesty?" the messenger, now quivering, asked.

"My pleasure? To have him executed for murder, what else? Why is he not here before me in chains? That's what I want to know. Did he walk the streets freely and no one in my command had the courage to arrest him?"

"The guards tried to seize him," the messenger said. "But they could not."

"Oh? And why couldn't they?"

The messenger shuffled his feet nervously. "He has some sort of . . . of magic, Sire."

"Magic!"

"Whenever the guards approached him, he held up his walking stick, and it . . ." The messenger hesitated as if he had difficulty believing what he was saying.

"Well?"

"It blinded them, Sire. With a terrible pain. Five of your soldiers have been taken to the hospital."

"Well, Nemathes?" the king asked. "Magic is your domain."

"I would have to see it to assess it, Majesty."

The king glowered at the messenger. "Where is he now?"

"Waiting in the Great Reception Hall. He has another man—his brother—and two boys with him."

Michelle sat up in her chair. "Danny and Wayne!" she exclaimed.

The king shot her a disapproving look and warned, "You'd do well to curb your excitement, my dear. If they are here for a treasonous purpose, I don't think you'd want to be numbered among them."

"Danny and Wayne wouldn't do anything like that," Michelle assured him.

"Let's meet them and see," the king said and strode out of the room.

In a long procession, they marched from the king's council chambers to the large reception hall near the front of the palace.

Michelle made eye contact with Danny and Wayne as soon as she entered the room. Their mouths went slack and their eyes bugged out at the sight of her. She smiled, pleased that they were surprised. She wondered if they might come over to talk to her, but they didn't. They remained a few steps off to the side of two tall men who also looked like brothers. One man had a beard, and the other was clean-shaven. Michelle guessed that the clean-shaven one was Fendar, but only because he carried the large walking stick.

The king did not look at Fendar or his company when he walked in. He went straight to his throne at the far end of the room and sat down. Only after a deafening silence did he lift his head and look at his former foster brother. "You have come back," he said. His voice was calm and betrayed none of the anger he'd shown in private.

Fendar bowed respectfully. "I have, Your Highness," he replied.

King Stefan observed to Nemathes, "At least he still acknowledges me as king."

"You *are* the king," Fendar said as he stepped closer. "And I come to you because you are a great king and have authority over this country."

Stefan raised his eyebrows. "You flatter me. What do you want? Clemency?"

"Mercy, Sire."

"Mercy! For whom, *you?* Have you come to ask the court's forgiveness for the murder you committed so many years ago?"

Fendar stiffened but made an effort not to be affected by the king's comments. He smiled coolly. Michelle was aware that she was watching an amazing performance by both men. The undercurrent of tension between them was so thick that you could have cut it with a knife.

"I have come to ask for mercy for my people."

Stefan laughed. "*Your* people! And who might *your people* be?"

"The Marutians."

"Do they acknowledge you as one of their own? You, an outcast, a murderer? Have they sent you to represent them? What has become of Regmund? He's the head elder. I speak only to him."

"My business with you isn't political but of a spiritual nature."

The king glared at him. "You jest. Have you become a priest during your years away?"

"I have come by the command of the Unseen One."

"The Unseen One is a Marutian notion. I don't believe in it."

"Nevertheless, the Unseen One laments that His chosen ones, the Marutians, no longer worship as they should."

"That has nothing to do with me. I never stopped them from worshiping their gods."

"The Unseen One would like me to take the Marutians out of the city and into the great forests to the north so they can learn to worship Him freely again, away from the influence of this city."

"Away from *my* influence, you mean."

"If you say so, Sire."

Stefan laughed again. "To take all the Marutians out of the city for a big summer worship camp would take days—days away from their work. My simple answer is no. If they want to worship anything, let them do it on their own time and in the privacy of their own homes."

Fendar was quiet for a moment, then said, "I have made the Unseen One's command to me a request to you, out of respect for you as king. But it remains a command. The

Unseen One wants His people back. Please let them go into the
forest with me—or suffer for your disobedience."

King Stefan stood up, his fists clenched with rage. "Are
you threatening me?"

"I say only what I am told to say."

"How dare you!" Stefan growled. "By what authority do
you, a fugitive, speak to me in this way?"

"The Unseen One Himself."

Nemathes suddenly stepped forward and said silkily, "Your
Highness, perhaps Fendar can offer us some proof of his
claims."

Fendar considered the challenge for a moment, then
turned to Wondrar and handed him the walking stick. "Throw
it down, brother," Fendar instructed.

Wondrar threw the stick onto the ground. To everyone's
astonishment, it turned into a hawk. It flapped its brown-and-
white wings and flew to the top of the giant crest on the wall
behind the throne. The hawk looked puny compared to the
gigantic eagle.

King Stefan applauded and said sarcastically, "How
delightful. Children's party tricks."

Nemathes approached the throne and, with a nod from the
king, picked up the king's scepter that had rested in a holder
nearby. It was gold, with a hollow crown on the top. Inside the
crown was a golden eagle. Nemathes closed his eyes and whispered something softly. Then he held the scepter upright in
front of the throne. Everyone gasped as the golden eagle
seemed to come to life, no longer gold but a bold black and
white. It screeched and flew to one of the throne's armrests.
Then a second eagle appeared at the top of the scepter—and a
third and a fourth—each one flying to the throne and perch-
ing on the armrests and the back.

Michelle watched this power play with amazement.

"How appropriate," Stefan said proudly as he stroked one of the eagles. "We have outnumbered your scraggly hawk with the eagle, our greatest symbol."

Nemathes then made a hissing noise and waved a finger at the eagles. They screeched loudly and flew toward the hawk as if to attack it.

Fendar held up his arm. Michelle thought he might be calling the hawk back for safety. But instead, the hawk stretched its wings and called out *kyah-kyah-kyah*. The wings fanned out wider and wider. Michelle blinked a few times to make sure she wasn't seeing things, because she thought the hawk was getting bigger and bigger. The eagles suddenly banked away with a furious flapping of wings and a flurry of feathers.

The hawk swooped to follow them, its enormous talons outstretched, and before anyone knew what was happening, it snatched one of the eagles from the air. The remaining three scattered. The hawk flew to the other end of the reception hall as the captive eagle let out a terrifying squawk. The hawk then dropped its prey. The eagle fell to the floor and hit with a sickening thud.

One of the members of the court ran to the fallen bird and picked it up. Its head flopped to one side. "Its neck has been broken!" the man cried.

While this was happening, the hawk swooped at another eagle, catching it in its great claws. Again the eagle screeched in a terrible panic, then went silent and fell to the ground. The hawk went after the third eagle and then the fourth, with the same results. Banking in the air above them all, the hawk flew to Fendar. But instead of lighting on his arm, the bird dropped to his outstretched hand. And the moment they touched, the hawk stood up straight and stiff and became a walking stick again.

"You will see us again," Fendar said to Stefan, and then he spun on his heels and walked out of the hall. Wondrar followed. Danny and Wayne lingered, as if they wanted to talk to Michelle, but they seemed to give up and followed the two men out.

Anger turned Michelle's cheeks red. The two boys had left her behind *again*. Didn't they care? The least they could have done was to come over and talk to her. Obviously they wanted to get rid of her, to go off on their own. They had probably planned it this way all along.

She seethed as she thought about it, but then she looked at the king and found herself feeling a smug satisfaction. This time they had picked the wrong side. They were hanging out with a murderer. They obviously didn't realize how powerful Stefan was.

The king didn't look so powerful at the moment, though. His face was ashen as he inspected the four dead eagles. Michelle was close enough to hear him tell Nemathes, "I want your spies to tell me his every move. When the time is right, I will arrest him and execute him for murder."

"Yes, Sire."

Stefan lowered his voice. "What is his power? It's more than magic."

Nemathes nodded and said, "I suspect the two children have brought it with them."

Stefan looked at Michelle out of the corner of his eye. "Do you have power, my child?" he asked.

"If they have power, I must have it, too," she guessed. "We came from the same place."

"It stands to reason," Nemathes agreed.

King Stefan pondered the thought, then leaned close to

Nemathes. "If she has power, we will need her to fight whatever Fendar brings against us." He turned to Michelle. "Will you help us fight against this murderer and rabble-rouser?"

"I'll do my best," she offered.

"But your cousins are with him," Nemathes observed.

Michelle shrugged. "That's their tough luck," she said confidently.

Stefan commanded Nemathes, "I want you to take care of this special lady. She is to have all the privileges of my court. I will look to her to advise me about Fendar."

Nemathes bowed again as Michelle grinned from ear to ear.

"What does she think she's doing?" Danny grumbled as they left the palace. They were riding in a wagon behind Fendar and Wondrar, who was driving the single horse that pulled them along.

"Maybe the king kidnapped her," Wayne suggested.

"She didn't look kidnapped," Danny countered. "Did you see how she was dressed? And she had that smug expression on her face. You know—the one she gets whenever she thinks she's right and we're wrong."

"Maybe they brainwashed her."

"Don't be so goofy."

"I'm not being goofy. Maybe we have to go back and rescue her." Wayne tapped Fendar on the shoulder. "Excuse me," he said, "but I'm really worried about our cousin."

"Don't be," Fendar replied over his shoulder. "She is exactly where she's supposed to be."

"But she's at the palace with the king. Isn't she supposed to be with us?"

Fendar shook his head. "If she's with us, she can't fulfill her part in the work of the Unseen One."

Danny slumped back. "You know what part she's supposed to play?"

"Yes."

"But how?"

"By keeping my eyes open."

"If you know her part," Wayne asked, "then what's *our* part?"

"You'll learn soon enough," Fendar answered. "Just wait and see."

CHAPTER SIX

Just a few hours later, things changed in the Promised Land. The news came while Fendar, Danny, and Wayne were having a late lunch at Wondrar's townhouse. Two small children, a boy named Maykar and a girl named Aintrar, played around their feet, and Wondrar's wife, Sainbry, had served them sandwiches and drinks when a knock came at the door.

"The king has proclaimed that we Marutians are obviously ungrateful to him," Regmund complained as he entered. He was clearly recovered from his earlier entanglements. "He has decided we must have too little to do if we think there's time to go off into the woods to worship, so he's adding an extra hour's work to our day. We have you to thank, Fendar."

"This is what I expected him to do," Fendar said calmly. "The Unseen One is prepared to persuade him."

"Persuade him how?" Regmund asked.

"That's up to Danny."

Danny nearly choked on his sandwich. "What?" he exclaimed.

"You will tell us how to persuade him."

"How am I supposed to know?" Danny asked.

"I suggest you consult with the Unseen One," Fendar answered.

Danny looked at him helplessly. "But—"

Fendar put a reassuring hand on his arm. "Finish your lunch, and then we'll take a walk together."

"Wait a minute!" Wayne protested. "How come *he* gets to decide? What about me?"

Fendar frowned at him. "You'll play your part at the right time. Be patient."

Wayne folded his arms and pouted. "I always have to be patient."

"What am I supposed to tell the people while your orphans decide their fates?" Regmund asked facetiously.

"Tell them to trust in the Unseen One," Fendar said and took a bite of his sandwich.

Not surprisingly, Danny lost his appetite completely. How was he supposed to know what to do? He fidgeted while Fendar finished eating. Fendar talked about family matters with Wondrar and Sainbry. They reminisced about their parents and compared notes about raising children. Then, finally, Fendar indicated that it was time for a stroll. Wayne continued to pout as they walked out the door.

They walked silently, gazing at the apartment buildings and townhouses of the Promised Land. Men and women walked past on the sidewalk. Some ignored them, others did a double take at Fendar, while others scowled at him outright. Fendar didn't seem bothered about it at all. About a quarter of an hour later, they passed through the gate into Muirk itself and headed for the city center. Danny wasn't sure where they were going, and Fendar didn't walk as if he had any particular place in mind. Looking around at the city, Danny was struck again by the majesty of the buildings and statues. *This is a city that's proud of itself*, he thought. *Only a people who know they're powerful would build a city like this.*

For no particular reason, the idea stayed with him. *The Palatians are powerful and proud*, he found himself thinking again and again.

They walked into a great park in the middle of the city. Horse trails and paths led them to a lake, at the head of which was a large structure with long stairs and with high pillars holding up the roof.

"It's a mausoleum," Fendar said as they drew closer. "The royal family is buried there."

"Even your adopted mother and father?" Danny asked.

"Even them."

Danny realized as they reached the foot of the steps that the building wasn't made of marble, as he'd thought at a distance, but of a white gold.

"Wow," Danny said, hardly believing it.

"The older generations of kings and queens believed that you must be buried in great splendor so that Death would be impressed when it came for your soul," Fendar explained. "They were also buried with gold coins in their pockets so they might bribe Death."

"*Bribe* Death?"

"Yes," Fendar said earnestly. "Bribe Death so it would take them to the realms of the gods."

They remained at the foot of the building. A sad darkness lingered behind the large pillars. Danny had no interest in going farther.

Fendar sighed deeply. "The gold for this building came from the mines of Marus. It was built by the blood and sweat of Marutians. My people built most of the newest and biggest buildings in this city. For what? For a small house and basic comforts in a ghetto they call the Promised Land. For the glory of dead kings and queens who brought nothing into this world when they arrived and could take nothing with them when they left." He paused and then added softly, "My people have forgotten that the Unseen One is the God of life. True life. Life beyond the comforts of this world. We were not made for this place, Danny."

Danny listened quietly, then asked, "What am I supposed to do, Fendar?"

"The Unseen One will tell you," Fendar answered.

"How?"

Fendar smiled. "You'll know."

They strolled back to the Promised Land. Once or twice, Danny thought he saw someone watching them from behind a tree or around the corner of an alley, but he dismissed it as his imagination. He had other things on his mind. He couldn't shake the terrible feeling that everything was riding on him, but he hadn't a clue about what to do.

Back at Wondrar's, more elders arrived throughout the evening to complain about the added work King Stefan was giving them the next day. Fendar insisted that it was all to a good purpose, that they would be freed to go home to Marus where they belonged. But no one seemed to hear him. Some of the elders said that Marus was now the home of jackrabbits, thieves, and nomads. It was not their home.

Fendar indulged their complaints with a weary smile and assured them that they would see and understand in due time.

"So, Mister High-and-Mighty, what's going to happen tomorrow?" Wayne asked Danny when they were back at the apartment and getting ready for bed.

Danny shrugged.

"You don't know?" Wayne snorted. "Some great leader you turned out to be."

"Leave me alone," Danny said sternly.

Danny turned the lamp down and crawled into bed. Wayne's cold feet were waiting for him. "Get off my side," Danny ordered in a low, threatening tone.

Wayne moved over a little. "I have plenty of ideas about

what Fendar can do to make the king change his mind," he declared.

"Good for you."

"I just don't understand why *you* get to decide. Just because you're the oldest, I'll bet. And you don't even know what to do."

"Just be quiet and go to sleep."

Wayne was quiet for a moment, then said, "I'd have Fendar call down lightning from heaven. Just like those guys in the Bible used to do. *Zap!* Then they'd be impressed."

"And what if the king's magicians can do the same thing?"

Wayne didn't answer at first. Danny hoped he had fallen asleep. "I'll bet they can't," Wayne finally said.

Danny groaned and rolled over. A light from somewhere outside shone through the curtains. Danny stared at it for the longest time. Someone must have eventually put it out, though, because at some point he was looking into darkness. It was the same kind of darkness he had seen behind the pillars at the mausoleum—a deep black that seemed to go back forever. Danny saw himself standing between those pillars, gazing into the mouth of the darkness. He could hear the sound of coins falling, as if someone were dropping them into someone else's palm. Was it the palm of Death? Was Death taking a bribe from the kings and queens?

Danny wanted to run away, but his bare feet moved forward. He felt gritty sand beneath his toes, as if he were walking on a beach. He glanced down and saw that he was walking on coins that were dissolving into dust. He felt as if he might sink and reached out to steady himself against a pillar. But the pillar cracked and then shook and moved. Danny feared it might collapse and bring the roof down on him. He stepped back. The steps beneath his feet also cracked, as if someone had dropped a huge rock onto thin ice.

Then a voice spoke from somewhere inside. It was calm and reassuring, unlike any he'd ever heard. It was neither high nor low in timbre, nor loud or soft. Yet it spoke clearly, as if in his ear, but from somewhere far away, too.

"Bring it down, one piece at a time," the voice said.

"What do you mean?" Danny asked.

"Piece by piece," the voice said. "One piece at a time."

The mausoleum shuddered and shook and began to collapse in on itself. Danny raced down the steps to get as far away as he could. He reached the edge of the lake and stopped. Two moons were reflected in the water.

"Two moons?" he asked out loud.

"What?" Wayne asked from the bed.

Danny turned. He was now standing at the window, looking out at the night sky. He had no idea how he'd gotten there. "Two moons," he said again.

Wayne got out of bed and saw what Danny was seeing: Two moons hung together in the sky.

"Whoa!" Wayne said, impressed.

Danny went back to bed. He now knew what had to be done to persuade the king. And he fell asleep right away.

CHAPTER SEVEN

Early the next morning, Danny took Fendar aside and told him about his dream and his thoughts concerning the signs. Fendar listened and nodded. "The Unseen One has spoken through you," he concluded.

Danny and Wayne went with Fendar and Wondrar back to the palace. The guards scowled at them but allowed them to go through without any interference. Because it was a gloriously sunny morning, the king was having breakfast with Nemathes and Michelle on a balcony that overlooked the rear gardens of the palace.

Michelle smirked at Danny and Wayne as the servant led them through the double doors onto the balcony. The silver on the coffeepots and cutlery gleamed in the sunshine.

"Well, look who's here," Michelle said in a voice meant to taunt them.

"I hope you've come up with something *really* big," Wayne whispered to Danny. "We have to show her."

"It's not a contest," Danny whispered back.

"Yes, it is," Wayne countered.

Wondrar nudged them to be quiet as Fendar bowed to the king.

"I hope you've given my request further consideration," Fendar said.

Stefan dabbed his mouth with a napkin. "I certainly have," he replied. "Your people will experience the results of my consideration all day today. They will work as they have never worked before."

"Then you will not let us leave?"

"No."

Fendar gazed at Stefan somberly. "Then you yourself have chosen to set into motion the signs of your own Ancient Oracles and the Sacred Writings."

"The Ancient Oracles spoke of three children. You have two. I have one. But I think this child"—he gestured to Michelle—"is equal to your two."

Michelle beamed at Danny and Wayne. Wayne growled softly.

Fendar turned to Danny.

Danny, realizing this was his cue, stepped forward to the king. He felt nervous and stammered through a dry voice, "The glory of Palatia will disappear before your very eyes before the morning is out."

"Oh, will it?" King Stefan replied with a smile.

"It will," Fendar said. "Then you will know that the Unseen One is more powerful than anything in which you place your hope. Gold and silver lead to ruin, but faith and obedience lead to everlasting life. You will let my people go free."

The king leaned forward on the table, the plates and cutlery rattling in response. "Fendar, your life is spared only because of my patience. Why am I patient? Because I admit to being curious about this game you're playing. I want to see how far you will take it." Stefan chuckled, low and without humor. "I remember when we played games as children. Just when you were on the edge of victory, you gave in. You pulled back to let the other side have a sporting chance. That's why you wouldn't have made a very good king."

Fendar looked down at the king, a staid expression on his face. "This isn't a game, Sire. And you would be unwise to treat it as such. Take what I say very, very seriously. The Unseen

One wants His people to know Him again. And they will."
Fendar leaned closer and added, "So will you."

Wondrar pulled a pouch of coins from his belt. They jingled
as he placed them on the table. Fendar then nodded to him,
and Wondrar lifted the walking stick until the very tip of it
touched the pouch.

"What does this mean?" Stefan asked.

"Pick it up, Sire," Fendar answered.

The king gestured for Nemathes to pick up the pouch. It
no longer jingled but hung heavy. Nemathes untied the top
and poured the contents onto the table. The coins inside had
turned to dust.

"Unless you let the Marutians go to worship the Unseen
One, all the wealth of the land will become as the coins in that
pouch," Fendar warned.

"Nemathes?" the king said.

Nemathes looked at Fendar with jaded eyes. He stood up,
shoved a hand into his vest pocket, and produced three shiny
coins. He sat them on the table and waved his hand over them.
They also turned to dust.

"More magic tricks," Stefan snorted.

"You'll see," Fendar warned. He nodded to Wondrar. They
turned and walked off.

Danny hesitated for a moment, his eyes fixed on Michelle.
"Please come with us," he requested.

"No way," Michelle replied. "You and Wayne should stay
here."

"Yes! I'd love to have you stay here at the palace," the king
affirmed, a teasing tone in his voice.

Wayne looked at Danny as if he thought they should agree.

"No, thank you," Danny said. "We don't belong here."

"Maybe *you* don't," Michelle snorted, "but *I* do."

"Suit yourself." Danny tugged at Wayne's sleeve, and they left the balcony.

Michelle watched them go. Why did they always have to be so stubborn? she pouted.

"I could have my guards stop them," the king offered, as if he knew what she was thinking.

Nemathes shook his head. "I don't believe Fendar would let you get away with that," he cautioned.

Stefan glowered at his adviser. "Let *me* get away with it? Am I not the king of this country?" He pushed his chair back angrily. "Nemathes, I'm beginning to think you *admire* Fendar."

"He has power, Sire," Nemathes said.

"Power to do what, a few magic tricks that you can mimic? I'm not impressed." The king frowned. "Did Fendar really think he could threaten me by turning a few coins into dust?"

The answer to King Stefan's question came later that morning. Michelle traveled with him and Nemathes to a meeting with the king's financial advisers at the Royal Bank of Palatia. When they arrived, the bank officials greeted the king with sweaty brows and panicked expressions.

"What's wrong?" the king asked, his voice echoing around the large, marbled reception area. Desks of tellers and accountants stretched out like boats on a sea.

The chief financial adviser was named Manticor and looked like a log with arms and legs. He bowed, wrung his hands, and replied, "Sire, something terrible has happened." He gestured for the king to follow him.

They navigated through the desks and around to another room. In it was a large, steel door to a vault. The door stood open, and the small party stepped inside. Michelle noticed right away the sound of some kind of sandy grit under the soles of her shoes.

"Look, Your Highness," Manticor said and pointed to the shelves. "Our supply of gold was kept on those shelves. But as you can see . . ."

A fine dust sat where there had been gold bars.

"Just like the coins this morning," Michelle whispered.

Nemathes shot her a disapproving look.

As if Manticor had heard her, he then went to a wall covered with units of small drawers. He began pulling them all out. "We kept coins in these drawers," he stated. He dropped his hand in one and produced a palm full of dust. "The coins have disappeared as well."

"What does this mean?" the king asked. "Were you robbed? Has someone replaced your gold with this dirt?"

"No, Your Highness. We have checked and double-checked that possibility. It's impossible for someone to have broken in, taken all our gold and bullion, and replaced it with this dirt. They would have had to spend hours and hours carting it in by the wagonload. It couldn't be done."

"Then explain it to me."

"I can't. It's as if everything has simply dissolved. But it's worse than that."

"Oh?"

"We have checked with the other banks. All *their* gold, silver, currency, reserves—*everything*—has turned to rubble."

The king began to pace around the vault, his fists clenched.

"This is a catastrophe of the highest order," Manticor said in a high, squeaky voice. "Our nation's wealth has disappeared. How will we buy or sell? How will we trade with other nations?"

King Stefan spun on the man. "Keep your wits, you fool!" he commanded. "Don't panic!" Then he turned to Nemathes. "Well? What do you have to say for yourself?"

Nemathes looked at him blankly. "Sire?"

"Fendar did this. We know he did. Now you have to fix it!"

"I don't understand, Sire."

"You mimicked Fendar's trick with the coins. You turned them to dust. Surely you must be able to undo the damage. Wave a magic wand. Turn this dust back into gold!"

"I can try, Your Highness."

"Don't try. You must *succeed*." With that, the king marched out of the vault, Manticor at his heels like a puppy.

Nemathes grabbed a large pouch of dirt that had held money until this morning. "We'll take this back to the palace to work on," he said. "I'll bring in my best magicians, my alchemists. Together we'll figure it out."

"Do you think you can do it?" Michelle asked.

Nemathes shoved his fingers into a pile of dirt and let it filter through. "Perhaps. If you have the power your cousins have, you can help me to reverse what they've done."

Michelle blushed as she felt put on the spot. "But I don't know how."

Nemathes suddenly grabbed her arm. "Your value to the king—and to me—is based on your ability to thwart Fendar," he said, his voice a dark rumble. "If you cannot do that, what use are you?"

Michelle had no answer for him.

Nemathes assembled all of Muirk's magicians and wizards at his workshop in the palace dungeon. The stone walls dripped with damp, and the floor was cold and wet. Wooden cabinets lined one wall, and several shelves cluttered with books and scrolls lined another. A large cage—almost like a man-sized birdcage—hung from the ceiling.

Michelle shivered as the strange crew, dressed in long, colorful robes adorned with stars and quarter-moons, gathered around various tables, each with some of the dirt that had once been gold. She watched in wonder as they tried numerous spells and incantations. One alchemist poured some of the dirt into beakers and cauldrons and added green and goopy ingredients that made her feel nauseated. Nothing worked. The dirt remained dirt.

Frustrated by their failure, Nemathes forced Michelle to try. But all she could think to do was to put her hands on the dirt and say things like "Abracadabra" and "Presto chango"— to no effect.

Eventually, as the afternoon became evening and everyone seemed bug-eyed from their efforts, Nemathes gave up. He put a hand on Michelle's shoulder and said ominously, "We'll talk to the king together."

Michelle felt nervous at first. But as they ascended from the dark cellars and made their way to the king's quarters, she began to feel an anger burn deep inside her. This was Danny and Wayne's fault. They had ditched her back at the fountain, and now they were determined to humiliate her at every turn. They had never liked her. Danny didn't really mean it when he'd asked her to join them. If he had, Fendar would have waved his walking stick and made the king let her go. Instead, they had left her to deal with their tricks on her own. One way or another, she'd get back at them, she concluded.

The king sat in a chair, his head held wearily in his hands. He looked up as Nemathes and Michelle entered.

"Well?" he asked.

Nemathes cleared his throat, then announced, "I regret to inform Your Highness that—"

Stefan held up his hand to silence Nemathes. "Don't continue. I know what you're going to say."

"My deepest apologies, Sire," Nemathes said softly.

"I'm sure you did your best, Nemathes," the king replied

with a worn smile. "You have been a good and loyal friend to
me all these years. If I speak harshly to you, it is only because
of my frustration."

"I know, Sire."

Waving them to sit down, the king continued, "I have
been all day with my financial advisers, trying to determine
how to avert a crisis throughout the country. I believe we've
come up with a plan, but it will be a difficult and slow process.
Already we've had riots in some of the townships." Stefan
looked at Michelle. "I have no doubt that my former brother
and your cousins are having a laugh at our expense."

Michelle imagined it: Danny and Wayne were laughing at
her until their sides ached. She clenched her teeth and said,
"But we won't let them get away with it, will we? I mean,
you're not going to give in, are you?"

"Of course not," the king said. "It will take more than this
to make me concede to Fendar."

"Good."

The king pondered Michelle for a moment, then observed,
"You are a determined child."

Michelle nodded. "My parents say I'm strong-willed."

"A strong will is what one must have to be a true leader,"
Stefan said approvingly. "It's what separates rulers from their
subjects. Remember that and you will go far in life."

"What will happen next, Sire?" Nemathes asked, changing
the subject back to their immediate problems.

"I will summon Fendar to the palace tomorrow. I want him
to know that his tricks have no effect on me." He suddenly
clapped his hands. A servant appeared in the doorway. "Bring
me the master of the workmen," the king commanded. "The
Marutians worked hard today, and they will work even harder
tomorrow."

CHAPTER EIGHT

———✦———✦———

A near riot erupted in the Promised Land the next morning. King Stefan's soldiers arrived at sunrise and began corralling men into large wagons. Many of them now carried whips, which they'd never had before, and used them on the backs of Marutian men. Regardless of what their previous jobs had been, the Marutians were taken away to harder assignments. Regmund came straight to the apartment and woke Fendar and the two boys by pounding on the door and shouting at the windows.

"Calm down, Regmund," Fendar said after letting him in. "What new assignments have the men been given?"

"To work in the mines!" Regmund shouted. "The king says he wants our people to find and replenish the supply of gold and silver that *you* turned to dust."

Wondrar, who came in while Regmund was speaking, remarked, "But no one has found gold or silver in Palatia's mines for decades."

"That's the whole point!" Regmund's face turned red as if his head might explode. "The king is punishing us for what you've done! His soldiers are *beating* our men. Now the people are complaining to me about it. What am I supposed to tell them?"

"I have prayed to the Unseen One about this," Fendar replied. "You have to tell the people to be patient. Tell them that as surely as *He* changed the Palatian money to dust, He is going to take them home."

"*If* there are any survivors to take home," Regmund lamented. "The king is going to work us all to death."

In a stern voice, Fendar asked, "Do you still doubt the power of the Unseen One?"

"It's not His power but your use of it that I doubt," Regmund stated.

Later, after Regmund left, a young boy came from Wondrar's house with a message. "The king is looking for you," he said breathlessly. "He has sent couriers all over the Promised Land to find you."

"To arrest me?"

"No," the boy explained, "he wants you to come to the palace."

"Maybe he's ready to give in," Danny suggested hopefully.

"Maybe he is," Fendar said, but he looked doubtful.

As they rode in the wagon through the streets of Muirk to the palace, Wayne told Danny, "I can't wait to see Michelle's face. I'll bet it blew her socks off when all their money turned to dust."

Danny didn't answer. He didn't feel as smug about it as Wayne, and he didn't like being on opposite sides from Michelle. Sure, she was a pain in the neck sometimes, but she was still their cousin and belonged with them. Danny also worried that the king might hurt her if he got mad enough at Fendar.

"What will you suggest if the king won't let the Marutians go?" Wayne asked.

Danny shook his head. "I'd better not say. It might mess things up somehow. I'll say what the next sign is when Fendar asks."

Wayne studied his brother for a moment. "You don't really know, do you?"

"Know what?"

"You don't know what the next sign is."

Danny looked away to watch the people on the street. They were crowded onto the sidewalks, hustling to wherever their jobs or responsibilities took them. Danny noticed that almost everyone was dressed in stylish clothes. Some were colorful, while others were simply smart-looking. Top hats bobbed up and down on the men's heads, and the women's dresses billowed bell-like in a kaleidoscopic display.

Wayne nudged him. "You don't know what the signs are, do you?"

"No, I don't," Danny admitted. "But somehow I get an idea. I can't explain it. It's like I get . . . inspired. And somehow, Fendar and Wondrar know it's right when I tell them. It's strange, but they look at me as if they suddenly had the same idea."

"That's weird," Wayne said.

King Stefan met them in the main reception hall. Many of the members of his court and his advisers were there. Michelle stood nearby, dressed in a robe of purple velvet, but she refused to look at either of the boys' faces. She maintained a stony expression, even when Danny tried to catch her eye. Nemathes stood next to her like a guard.

"Well, Fendar, I hope you are satisfied," the king said.

"Satisfied, Your Highness?"

"Many of your people will leave Muirk for a day in the country, as you requested," Stefan replied.

"To work in the mines, digging for something they won't find," Fendar countered.

The king chuckled. "If you're going to be picky about it . . ."

"You won't set my people free?" Fendar asked.

"Why should I?"

"Because the Unseen One commands it."

"Ah, yes, the Unseen One commands it. The all-powerful Unseen One who caused that minor inconvenience yesterday."

"Taunt me if you must, but beware of what you say about Him," Fendar warned.

"I am the king here!" Stefan suddenly shouted. "Don't you dare tell me what I may or may not say!"

Fendar bowed respectfully. "I won't argue with you. Since you refuse to heed the Unseen One, there is another message from Him."

Again, it was Danny's turn to speak. He began, "The glory of Palatia will—"

"Disappear," the king interrupted. "You said so yesterday."

"You wear your vanity like rich robes," said Wondrar. "But they are rags in the sight of the Unseen One. Watch and know that the Unseen One alone is all-powerful." Wondrar then lifted the walking stick, and a blinding light dazzled them all. When Danny could see clearly again, he gasped—along with everyone else in the room.

The king's clothes, Michelle's robe, the clothes worn by everyone in the court—even the tapestries and curtains that hung from the walls—all were turned to stained and tattered rags. Only the clothes worn by Fendar, Wondrar, Danny, and Wayne remained as they had been.

Along with the change in clothes, a terrible smell filled the room. People put their hands to their mouths and coughed violently in response.

King Stefan couldn't hide his surprise. "What have you done?" he cried out.

Nemathes quickly stepped forward, his own garment hanging from him in ugly strips. "This is an old spell," he said confidently. He held out his arms, closed his eyes, and muttered to himself. Then he crossed and uncrossed his arms three times in rapid succession. There was another bright flash of light, and everything in the room returned to the way it had been. The clothes, the curtains, and the tapestries were all as good as new. The smell disappeared, too.

Danny was flabbergasted. *Nemathes had reversed the sign!*

"Uh-oh," Wayne said.

Now, for the first time that day, Michelle looked at Danny and Wayne. She smiled that irritating smile of hers. "Ha!" she said.

"Well done, Nemathes!" the king shouted.

Danny looked up at Fendar and Wondrar. Wondrar, he noticed, looked worried. But Fendar was his usual calm self. He didn't speak or do anything. He seemed to be waiting for something to happen.

Then it did. Starting at the necks and shoulders of everyone's coats, shirts, and dresses, an ugly brown stain worked through the cloth. Holes appeared, and seams were torn as if by unseen hands. Downward the terrible change continued, passing through waistcoats and belts, consuming trouser legs and finally the bottoms of the shoes on everyone's feet. The tapestries became frayed, the crest of the eagle fading and unraveling from the fabric. The curtains became moldy. Even the cushions on the chairs faded and then exploded their stuffing like popcorn. The awful smell returned. People gagged and coughed.

Undaunted, Nemathes held out his arms, closed his eyes, muttered an incantation, and then crossed and recrossed his arms. Nothing happened. He tried again. Still nothing happened. He tried once more, this time frantically. It didn't work.

The king was trying to speak, but he couldn't because he was coughing too hard.

Only Fendar's clear voice could be heard now. "Set my people free!" he commanded, then turned to leave.

Danny and Wayne followed Fendar and Wondrar out, the sound of coughing ringing in their ears. They had to cup their hands over their noses and mouths to keep the stench away. Danny turned at the door for one last look at Michelle, but she was doubled over, taken by a fit of coughing. He felt bad leaving her behind again.

All the way down the palace halls, Danny could see the decay in anything made of fabric. The guards were looking themselves over with bewilderment.

The city of Muirk was caught up in chaos as the people ran into the streets. Men and women raced to and fro, as if trying to get somewhere—home, perhaps—to change out of their embarrassing outfits. Others stopped to compare their rags and discuss what had happened. Some stopped and got sick onto the pavement because of the smell.

The Palatian flags that had hung so proudly from the many royal buildings were now tattered and shredded.

When Fendar's group returned to the apartment in the Promised Land, Danny noticed that the clothes of the Marutians —and the curtains and cloth covering the furniture—were all intact. The air was free of the awful smell. The sign didn't seem to affect the Marutians at all.

"Even while it was happening, I wondered what this will accomplish," Wondrar told his brother once they were behind closed doors again.

"It will help to persuade King Stefan to let us go home. Sooner or later, our presence here won't be worth the inconvenience we'll cause. Even now, all of Palatia's fabric and clothes makers will be horrified to find that their best materials have turned into filthy rags. The whole nation is reacting to the terrible stench. Palatia has always been a nation of vain people. Now it has turned against them."

Later that afternoon, King Stefan met with nearly a dozen of his advisers, along with Nemathes and Michelle, in the gardens behind the palace. It was the only place where the smell of rotten cloth didn't overwhelm them.

"Losing our money was bad enough," one of the advisers complained. "But *this*—" He gestured to the rags hanging limp from his body.

The others agreed. "There's no escaping," one silver-haired man said. "At our offices, at home, in the public buildings, it's the same."

"Can't we negotiate with Fendar?" someone asked.

King Stefan looked off to some distant point in the garden. Michelle thought he seemed distracted.

"What does he want?" the silver-haired man asked. "A few days in the woods with the Marutians? If that's all he wants, we should grant it."

"Anything to stop this nonsense," another adviser concurred.

The king regarded them silently for a moment, then asked, "Is this what my advisers suggest? Shall we capitulate to his demands?"

"It isn't capitulation, Sire," the silver-haired man said. "You are merely showing your benevolence to your servants."

The king frowned. "Is that how you'll present it to the public? The king is not giving in out of weakness but out of strength?"

"Yes."

Stefan pondered the idea. Somewhere a bird sang. Michelle

watched the king, wondering what he would decide. She wanted to speak but was afraid to in this crowd. Was it her place? Suddenly, the king took the choice out of her hands. He turned to her and asked, "What do *you* think, Michelle?"

Michelle swallowed hard and said, "Me? Well, I think it's the principle of the thing."

"What do you mean?"

"I mean, it's like playing 'chicken.'"

"Chicken?"

"It's a game we play back in Odyssey. Two people will ride toward each other on their bicycles, and the first one to move out of the way is the chicken—the coward. The idea is to see who'll flinch first. Whoever does is the loser. If you give Fendar what he wants, you'll be the loser."

Nemathes, who had been quiet through the entire meeting, now raised an eyebrow and stated, "I might agree if we were playing a childish game. But we have lost our nation's wealth and now the clothes on our backs. This is not about winning or losing. It's about the survival of our people."

"No," the king suddenly said, his face alight, "Michelle is right. This *is* about winning and losing. I said as much myself to Fendar this morning. If I give in to him, I may as well abdicate as your king. He is strong, but I am stronger."

Michelle felt a deep satisfaction that the king had agreed with her. This was the way to go, she knew for sure. If Danny and Wayne got the better of her, there'd be no enduring them in the future.

Nemathes began, "But Sire—"

"Nemathes," the king interjected, cutting him off, "I would be more impressed with your advice if you backed it up with power. Where is your magic? Why haven't you been able to counter this mischief of Fendar's?"

"I have tried, Sire," Nemathes replied. "Even now, my magicians are experimenting with various incantations and spells."

"Then I'll be happy to hear from you when you have results."

"Yes, Your Highness," Nemathes said miserably.

The king held out his hand toward Michelle and declared to the entire assembly, "You would all do well to show the courage of this young girl. There is no doubt that she has been sent by the fates to guide me during this time."

Michelle blushed.

The king continued, "We must persevere. Whatever Fendar brings against us, we must stand firm against him." With that, he dismissed them all. Just as Michelle was about to go back into the palace, the king indicated that he wanted her to wait. After everyone had left, including a suspicious Nemathes, the king said, "I think I understand your purpose here."

"You do?"

"You have been sent to be my heart," the king explained softly. "You have an uncommon strength. I shudder to think of how formidable Fendar would be if he had the two boys *and* you on his side. But I see in you my chance to win in this contest of wills."

Michelle curtsied. "Thank you, Your Highness," she said, smiling broadly. Even in smelly rags, she felt like a princess.

CHAPTER NINE

———————

"Sire," Fendar greeted, bowing before King Stefan. Wondrar stood next to Fendar regally, his hand resting on the top of the walking stick. It was the next morning, and they were gathered in the reception hall. Danny was astounded to see the entire court still looking like vagabonds, dressed as they were in their rotten rags. Flies buzzed around them.

Wayne nudged Danny and pointed toward Michelle. "Look, she's dressed in her Odyssey clothes again," he whispered.

Sure enough, Michelle had on the pullover shirt, jeans, and sneakers she had worn to Trickle Lake. "She must've put them on because they aren't affected by the latest sign," Danny observed.

"How long will this tiresome game go on?" the king asked, looking less kinglike in his tattered robe.

"Until you allow the Marutians to worship freely," Fendar stated. He clasped his hands in front of him like a father whose patience is wearing thin. "What is your answer?"

"I thought working in the mines was answer enough," Stefan said.

"Then you are still unmoved?" Fendar asked.

"I will not accede to your demands, if that's what you mean. But I have a few demands of my own, including longer work hours. I see now that I've been far too permissive with the Marutians."

Fendar lowered his head. "So be it."

Danny knew, though he wasn't sure how he knew, that it was time for him to speak once more. He stepped forward and said, "The glory of Palatia will fade before your eyes. As a sign of the power of the Unseen One, your beauty will shrivel and itch and burn."

Wondrar then banged the bottom of the walking stick on the ground three times. He turned and walked out. Fendar followed him. Danny and Wayne, never sure when it was actually time to leave, hesitated, then went with the two men.

The king was surprised. "Is that it?" he asked Nemathes, who stood nearby.

Nemathes shrugged. "I don't know, Sire," he admitted.

The king leaned back on his throne and scratched at something on his neck. Many of his courtiers and servants were doing the same. It was subtle at first, as each person tried to be discreet, and then the whole room was active with movement. They scratched behind their ears . . . their noses . . . their chests . . . and their arms and legs. Michelle watched them, baffled and amused. She would have laughed if a woman hadn't suddenly screamed. She was pointing at the man standing next to her. His face was covered with pink and purple blotches. Everyone in the crowd turned to one another as shouts and cries rose up. Something terrible was happening. They scratched and scratched while their skin went painfully red.

"Nemathes, do something!" the king shouted as he dug at his own flesh.

Nemathes stepped forward and, after shouting words Michelle didn't understand, waved his arms. Whatever he had hoped to accomplish had no effect.

Michelle stepped back toward the wall as people stumbled and fell past her. Most were clawing for the door, hoping to escape somehow. Michelle looked down at her own hands and arms, but no blotches appeared. And apart from feeling itchy out of sympathy for everyone around her, she didn't suffer from this latest sign. "I must be immune," she said softly, which was exactly what she had said the night before when she'd discovered that her Odyssey clothes were unaffected.

"Somebody do something!" the king commanded. He had fallen to his knees in front of his throne, scratching at his chest and legs while he rubbed his back against the armrest.

For Wayne, the ride back to the Promised Land was comic. He couldn't help but giggle at the people in the street as they went through wild contortions to deal with their itching. For Danny, though, it was horrifying to watch. He prayed that this time King Stefan would give in. In his heart, though, he knew that it was going to get worse. *A lot* worse.

Danny also worried about Michelle. Was she afflicted with the skin disease, or was she safe?

Wayne seemed to be thinking about the same thing. "I'd love to see Michelle squirming around like that," he chuckled as he jabbed an elbow into Danny's side.

Danny pushed him away. "Grow up, will you?" he chided.

"Hey, what's your problem?" Wayne asked defensively.

"It's not funny," Danny explained. "This is serious business."

Wayne scowled at his brother and then pouted for the rest of the ride.

Regmund and the rest of the elders met their wagon at the gates of the Promised Land. They wanted to have a meeting right away, Regmund said. Fendar agreed.

Danny was prepared to go with them, but Fendar stopped him. He pulled both boys close and whispered, "You don't have to come. This is going to be a long and boring argument, just like the others. They're going to complain about how hard they have to work and how it's all my fault and how they wish I would leave things alone."

"And what are you going to tell them?" Danny asked.

"I'm going to explain that freedom is never free. It must be bought with sacrifice and, sometimes, great pain."

"But what if they don't want freedom?" Danny asked.

"The desire to be free rests deep within the hearts of all men and women. Sometimes, however, that desire is lulled to sleep. It's my job to awaken it again. When all of this is done, the Marutians will remember who they are, and they'll rise up."

"The elders are getting impatient," said Wondrar.

Fendar acknowledged him and the two of them went off to the assembly room.

"So what do you want to do?" Danny asked Wayne. For the first time since they'd arrived in this strange world, they had time to themselves.

Wayne was still in a sulky mood. "Nothing with *you*," he said and walked off.

Danny watched him go. He thought about following him to talk about what was wrong. Then he decided it would be better to keep his distance. Something more pressing occupied his mind. He looked around and made his way toward Muirk.

Nemathes called together all the chemists and apothecaries in the city. They brought to the palace their various ointments and creams, and eventually they found a way to soothe the itching and burning. But they couldn't do anything for the way people looked. The red, pink, and purple blotches covered everyone's bodies. They were repulsive to the eye. Michelle found herself looking down at the carpet, the paintings on the palace walls, or *anywhere* other than at the faces of the men and women around her.

"He's gone too far," an adviser named Penwyth told the king. He was a stately old gentleman who spoke with candor and authority. "If this continues, you will lose the support of the upper classes. We can't bear to look at one another like this." The others in the group, mostly men and women of the upper classes Penwyth had mentioned, muttered their agreement.

"What are you advising?" the king asked testily.

"Let the *confounded* man take his *confounded* people out into the *confounded* woods!" Penwyth said. "Once they get this nonsense out of their system, they'll come back and we can put things right again."

The others again murmured their assent.

The king looked at Michelle. She averted her gaze. She still felt the king shouldn't give in, but she didn't want to push her luck. To say so in this crowd might get her in trouble. She glanced up, and the king was still looking at her. He wanted to know what she thought. She slowly shook her head.

The king leaned forward in his throne. "So my aristocracy can't bear the *inconvenience* brought about by Fendar's antics?" he challenged. "It's too much for them, is it?"

His tone was so thick with sarcasm that no one dared to answer.

"I won't consider it!" he said as he slapped his hand on the throne's armrest. "We are fighting for the rights of all Palatians. If we let this one man walk all over us now, how can we hold our heads up in the future? What will our children say? Will we be remembered as those who overcame the belligerence of the Marutians, or will they spit on our graves as those who caved in to an inferior people? No! I won't entertain the idea of giving Fendar what he wants."

The king dismissed the advisers. As they left, a servant slipped in and whispered something in Nemathes's ear.

Nemathes nodded and then cautiously approached the throne. "Sire, may I have a word with you?" he asked.

"What is it, Nemathes?"

Nemathes leaned close to the king, who listened, then nodded and glanced at Michelle.

"You're looking pale, Michelle," the king said. "I would like you to take a walk in the garden."

Michelle was struck by the suddenness of the king's suggestion. "You want me to take a walk . . . right this minute?"

"It would be good for you."

Michelle then realized what the king wanted. "Oh, I get it. You want to talk to Nemathes alone."

The king smiled. "You are a shrewd child. So, if you don't mind . . ."

Michelle felt a little hurt that she was being left out, but she said, "Yes, Sire. If that's what you want."

"It will serve our purposes well, thank you."

Michelle walked out of the reception hall and down the long corridor that led to the rear of the palace. It seemed empty and hollow to her. The banners and tapestries hung in strips from the walls. Servants passed by with their heads held low and their faces covered. She stepped out through the doors that led onto the large rear porch, then down the long steps to the gardens. It was another bright summer's day. The flowers and trees were untouched by the chaos Fendar had created everywhere else. *Maybe the king was right,* Michelle thought as she took a deep breath. *Maybe I needed a walk.*

The lawn stretched out as far as she could see. Circular designs of pavement and flowers led up to a large fountain. Off to the left and the right were trimmed hedgerows and patches of flowers placed in colorful patterns. Dotted throughout were benches so that people could sit and enjoy the views. She found a bench well away from the palace itself and sat down. A bird sang in a bush nearby. The sound of the splashing fountain caused her mind to wander.

She thought about the events that led up to where she was now. Not so long ago, she was just a kid wandering around a hippie festival at Trickle Lake. Now she was like an adviser to a king—his *guru*. Apart from Nemathes, she might be one of the most powerful people in the whole country!

"Pssst!"

Michelle turned around quickly.

"Over here," came a whisper.

She looked toward a collection of tall bushes that had been designed as a giant maze. A small, wooden sign said the maze was called The King's Labyrinth. Beneath that, it said:

A-*maze* yourself with this royal delight;
Delight yourself with this royal a-*maze*.
Lose yourself with a friend or a foe;
Find your way or ne'er be found.
But don't despair when the hours wane;
Look up! Look up!
The King's Passage will lead you home.

"Here!" came the whisper again. A hand waved at her from the opening to the maze.

Michelle now saw who it was. "Danny!" she cried out.

"Keep your voice down!" he snapped.

Michelle got up from the bench and went over to him. "Are you alone?" she asked. "What are you doing here?"

"I came to see you," he replied.

"What for?"

"I was worried about you. I thought maybe the skin disease might have . . . you know . . . hurt you."

"Your stupid signs don't affect me." Michelle looked around quickly. "You must be crazy to come here without Fendar. If King Stefan or Nemathes sees you, you'll be locked up."

"Why do you think I hid out here? I was hoping you might decide to take a walk. Otherwise, I was going to sneak into the palace and try to find your room."

"You'd never find it without knowing where it is."

Danny glanced at Michelle nervously. "Michelle, I've got this feeling that everything's going to get a lot worse. You need to come with me. Right now."

"You're kidding."

"No. You're not going to be safe here for very long."

"I'm a lot safer than you are. When King Stefan gets tired of all this fooling around, he's going to come down really hard on Fendar and the whole bunch of you."

"He may try, but he won't succeed. The Unseen One is powerful, Michelle."

Michelle grunted her disbelief.

"I don't understand you," Danny said, taking a different tack. "You're the one who was against everybody in authority. Teachers, politicians, parents—they were all out to oppress us, you said."

"They're out to oppress *me*, I said."

"So what about King Stefan?"

"What about him?"

"He's oppressing people."

Michelle turned her nose up proudly. "He's not oppressing *me*. He asks me what I think. He listens to me."

"Oh, I get it now. He's made you a big shot, and now you're

happy to go along with whatever he wants. Is that it?" Danny shook his head woefully. "I'll bet to top it all off, you have a crush on him."

"I do not!" Michelle protested.

"Then what about all those things you made such a big deal about? You talked my ear off about freedom and rights. What about the freedom and rights of the Marutians?"

Michelle gazed at Danny as if he'd asked a stupid question. "They have plenty of freedom and all kinds of rights. King Stefan tells me that even the wealthiest people of other countries don't have it as good as the Marutians do here. Until Fendar came along, they worked at jobs that suited them and lived in nice homes."

"But they're still *slaves*. No matter how good Stefan makes it for them, they're slaves. They're not free and they don't have any rights. They can't even go out into the woods to worship the Unseen One."

"As I understand it, none of them really want to go out to worship the Unseen One. It's Fendar who's trying to make them do it."

"That's because King Stefan keeps confusing them."

"Or maybe Fendar is the one who's confusing everybody."

"Fendar is the only one who knows what's going on. He's in touch with the Unseen One. He's going to wake the Marutians up to who they really are, and he's going to free them from Stefan. Nothing will stop him."

"Ha!"

"Listen to me, Michelle. *Please.* The Unseen One brought us here from Odyssey. But He brought us over to help Fendar, not the king. Come with me now, and maybe when this is all over, we can go home again. Don't you want to go home?"

"Not especially. I like it here."

Danny growled. "You're just like the Marutians! King Stefan has duped you."

"You're the one who's duped, Danny," Michelle said with a snooty tone. "After the king defeats Fendar, you and Wayne are going to be left out in the cold. You might get locked up as traitors. Then what're you going to do? I may not be able to help you then. But if you come into the palace now and tell the king you'll help him . . ."

"No. We don't belong here."

"I know what your problem really is," Michelle said. "You just don't like it that a girl is more powerful than you. You're such a chauvinist."

"And you're pathetic," Danny said.

Just then, they heard a rustling around the hedges, out of sight. Danny turned to look and saw two guards appear. "Uh-oh," he said. He spun to run in the other direction, but two guards were rounding that corner, too.

"Get him!" one of the guards shouted.

With nowhere left to run, Danny retreated into the maze.

"What's going on here?" Michelle shouted at the guards as they raced in after Danny. "Leave him alone!"

From behind her, Nemathes said, "Well done, Michelle. The king will be very proud of you if we catch him."

"You knew he was here," Michelle said, suddenly realizing why the king had insisted she take a walk. "Someone saw Danny in the gardens, and that's why you sent me out."

"You are a clever girl." Nemathes smiled, his face puffed and swollen from the blotches. He patted her on the shoulder.

Michelle moved away from him. She didn't like to be tricked. And even though she thought Danny was wrong, she didn't want him caught and put in jail.

With the guards hot on his tail, Danny ran up and down

the various rows, around corners, into dead ends, and back out again without knowing where he was going or if he was even going in the right direction. Occasionally a guard shouted to another guard, which helped Danny more than it helped them. He soon realized that they didn't know the maze any better than he did. He tried to cut through the hedges, but they were thick, with pinlike needles on their branches. He tried to climb up and over one hedge, but the branches buckled under his weight, the needles stabbing into him.

"Get out of there!" Nemathes finally shouted irritably at the guards. "We'll surround the maze and catch him when he comes out. Now hurry up and go for reinforcements!"

Danny froze where he was, all hope disappearing fast. If he was going to escape, he had to do it before the reinforcements arrived. He could hear the guards in other parts of the maze, and it sounded as if they couldn't find their way out.

"How do we get out of here?" one of the guards yelled.

"You baboons!" Nemathes yelled back. "If I tell you, *he'll* hear. Just think of the *sign!*"

"Sign?" the guard asked. "What sign?"

Nemathes growled loudly in exasperation.

The sign? Danny wondered. At first he thought of Fendar's signs, but he knew that wasn't what Nemathes was talking about. Then he remembered the wooden sign at the front of the maze. What did it say? Danny had read it when he'd first arrived, but now he was hard-pressed to bring it to mind. Something about delight and a-*maze* and getting lost and friends and foes and . . . and . . .

King's Passage? That was it. It had said that if you were in despair, then do something about the King's Passage. But what was he supposed to do? Danny closed his eyes, trying to picture the sign. What did it say about the King's Passage?

Look up!

Danny looked up at the clear, blue sky. What was he supposed to see? He lowered his eyes until they rested on the tops of the hedges. He still didn't see anything. He allowed his gaze to follow the line of the solid row of hedges on his left, down to the end of the aisle. Then he noticed the top of the last bush wasn't flat but curved. He studied it, trying to make out the significance of the difference. Suddenly it came to him: That bush was sculpted to look like the top of a king's crown! He ran to it and had the choice of going left or right. To the left was a regular flat bush, and to the right was another curved bush. He raced in that direction. At every intersection or possible turning, one bush indicated which way to go.

More than once, Danny found himself only a hedge away from one of the guards. He could hear the guard on the other side of the greenery, sometimes kicking the dirt in anger, sometimes cursing.

After a few minutes, Danny reached an opening that led out of the maze. He approached it slowly, sure that Nemathes or a guard would be waiting for him. To his surprise, he'd come back to the entrance of the maze, not the exit. No one was there. They'd probably gone to the exit to wait for him.

Danny ran to the left. The guards still shouted from inside the maze, and he could hear Nemathes farther off. *Where's Michelle?* he wondered. He retraced his steps from how he'd originally come into the gardens, following the outside of the maze around to the north. He sprinted across to a thick forest to the west. That would lead to the tree with the long branch over the palace wall and Muirk beyond.

He was back in the Promised Land by the time the sun went down.

"Where have you been?" Fendar asked angrily when Danny returned to the apartment.

Danny stammered for a moment, aware of the trouble he'd be in if Fendar knew he'd gone back to the palace. He was tempted to tell a half-truth like "I took a walk," but he knew better. "I went to the palace to see Michelle," he finally admitted.

Fendar glared at him. "Have we come this far for you to jeopardize your life—or the Unseen One's purposes?" he demanded.

"No, sir."

Wayne stood nearby with a pleased expression on his face.

"Then what were you thinking?"

"I was worried about Michelle," Danny confessed. "I wanted to try and talk her into coming back here with us."

"That was stupid," Wayne said.

"Yes, it was," Fendar agreed.

Wayne's smile grew bigger.

"Stupid," Fendar repeated, though now his tone softened. "But understandable."

Wayne's face fell. Danny looked up at Fendar, astonished.

Fendar's eyes were filled with sadness. "You still don't seem to grasp that Michelle is fulfilling her role as she should. She is accomplishing the Unseen One's bidding."

"But she's on the *wrong side* and she thinks she's *right*," Danny said. "It's like she's gone power-crazy. She thinks she's one of the king's advisers. I'll bet she's even telling him not to listen to you."

"Then she is working within the will of the Unseen One."

"But I don't think she knows she's working within His will. She's doing it because it's the way she is," Danny said, then stopped to think if what he'd just said made any sense.

Fendar understood what he meant in any case, because he

replied, "The Unseen One often uses our own wrongheaded inclinations to accomplish His purposes."

"Do you mean the Unseen One *wants* her to work against us—and for the king to refuse to do what you want?"

"Perhaps. We may not know until we reach the end. But I promise you this: The Unseen One will not be thwarted. One way or the other, He'll do what He wants." Fendar paused to give Danny a chance to ask any more questions. Danny didn't know what to say. Fendar slapped his hands together. "Let's see about dinner."

The meal was a joyless affair. Though Fendar did his best to keep the mood light, Danny was lost in his thoughts about Michelle, and Wayne was pouting again.

That night as they were going to sleep, Wayne finally broke his cold silence and told Danny, "I know how Michelle feels. I'd probably do the same thing she's doing if I were in her shoes."

Danny sat up on his elbows and looked at his brother's shadow in the darkness. "You would?"

Wayne was quiet for such a long time that Danny thought he'd fallen asleep. But then Wayne continued, "You're the oldest, so you can't understand what it's like. But for Michelle and me, it's tough. We have to sit back and watch while you older kids get to do all the fun and important stuff. So it means a lot when someone treats us special."

"I don't get to do all the fun and important stuff," Danny argued.

Wayne clucked his tongue. Danny imagined he'd rolled his eyes, too. "I told you you couldn't understand."

Danny lay back again and sighed. "Okay. Maybe we do

sometimes. But we also have to do things we *don't* like. Mom and Dad, not to mention teachers—they always give me more responsibility than they give you. And they always say it's because I'm the oldest."

"Yeah, but it's still not fair," Wayne complained. "I'm supposed to be one of the three children everyone is talking about, but I haven't been allowed to do anything. When will I get my turn?"

Danny thought about it a moment, then said, "Probably when you least expect it."

CHAPTER TEN

❧————————❧

Their days now followed a routine. Danny and Wayne would get up, have breakfast with Fendar, be joined by Wondrar, and the four of them would ride in a wagon to the palace. The guards, who had never been friendly to them anyway, would grunt and wave them on. A servant would then lead them to wherever the king was holding audience. After the audience with the king, Fendar would meet with some of the Marutians to discuss their plight. He would then sneak away to be alone. Danny got the impression he went off to pray, sometimes for hours.

This morning, the king was in a particularly foul mood. Little wonder, since his clothes were falling off his back and his skin was covered with sores. But he remained fiercely stubborn and greeted the four with a terse "No."

"No, Sire?" Fendar inquired.

"Allowing the Marutians to leave Muirk is out of the question. How many times do I have to say it?"

"As you wish," Fendar answered, then waved Danny forward.

"The glory of Palatia will fade before your very eyes," he began.

"Like you did yesterday," the king interjected. "You disappeared before the eyes of my guards."

Danny cleared his throat and continued, "Money, fashion, and beauty are gone. Now watch what happens to your great industries."

Wondrar took the walking stick and casually strolled over

to one of the thick pieces of timber that made up the wall of
the reception hall. He tapped the stick against it and then
returned to Fendar's side.

"Know that the Unseen One is powerful throughout the
land of Palatia," Fendar said.

Everyone watched and waited to see what Wondrar's simple
action would mean. The king, whose hands had been grasping
the armrests of his throne, suddenly lifted them up. "What is
this?" he gasped as he stared at the wood on the armrests.

Nemathes came quickly to his side. "Sire?" he asked.

"The wood is rotting!" the king said, unable to take his
eyes off his throne.

"Throughout your kingdom," Fendar announced, "the
great Palatian trees, on which the renowned Palatian lumber
trade depends, will rot."

The palace began to creak like an old ship as the wood
started to fulfill Fendar's statement. The timber around them
turned from brown to an ashen gray. The court buzzed; then the
members moved to the doors, fearful that the roof might cave in.
Nemathes leaned toward the king and whispered in his ear.

Danny looked for Michelle. She stood off to the side of the
room. She hadn't moved and wouldn't look at him. Her expression, Danny thought, was pensive. Danny was disappointed.
He'd hoped that because she'd helped him at the maze yesterday, she might have had a change of heart.

Fendar indicated it was time to go. The two men turned,
with Danny and Wayne ready to follow, when the king suddenly shouted at them to stop.

That brought the chaos in the room to a standstill.

The king nodded to Nemathes, who crossed the room to
Fendar. "Fendar, you acted before the king had a chance to finish his statement," he said silkily.

"Oh?" Fendar said in obvious surprise.

"While it is not possible for your Marutians to leave Muirk to worship the Unseen One, there is another way."

Fendar waited for Nemathes to continue.

"The king would like to declare a national day of worship for everyone in Palatia. He will grant the Marutians complete freedom to have a feast in their district, with the assistance of the king himself, to worship the Unseen One here in Muirk."

This seemed like a reasonable counteroffer, Danny thought, and he wondered if Fendar would accept it.

Fendar looked past Nemathes and spoke to the king directly. "Sire, your offer seems kind," he stated diplomatically. "But it is like asking locked-up prisoners to celebrate their freedom without leaving their jail cells. You must let my people go free from Muirk to worship according to the Unseen One's commands."

King Stefan's face, purple and blotchy as it was, went a deep crimson. He stood stiff as a board, as if holding his breath and counting to 10 to control his anger. Then he turned away from them all. Michelle stepped forward anxiously. It looked to Danny as if she wanted to say something but didn't dare. Then, without facing them, the king said, "All right. Go where you want. Just put an end to these curses."

The members of the court gasped in surprise. Nemathes's eyes grew wide. Danny wanted to shout. Wayne even started to leap up, but Danny put a restraining hand on his brother's arm. Success at last!

Fendar and Wondrar exchanged glances. Neither of them looked satisfied or jubilant. In fact, they looked downright worried, Danny thought.

Fendar stepped forward and bowed. "What did Your Highness say?" he asked.

The king spun on his heel and repeated through clenched teeth, "Your Marutians may go out to worship for a few days. End your curses now."

Fendar, with no sign of relief, responded, "As you wish."

Wondrar held up the walking stick and then brought it down hard on the floor. It crashed with a thunderous sound, and a blinding light made them all shield their eyes. After a moment, the light subsided and Danny, blinking, looked around.

Everyone's skin had returned to normal. Everyone's clothes had changed from rags to the rich-colored fabrics they had been before. The crests and banners hung proudly once again. The timber was brown and firm. The king slumped down in his throne, now rot-free and sturdy again, and stared out a nearby window. He then moved his hand in a gesture so subtle that it was hard to see he'd even done it.

Nemathes saw it, however, and immediately clapped his hands loudly. "The king wishes to be alone. You are dismissed!" he ordered.

Danny had no doubt that the king felt humiliated. Everyone left the reception hall in silence. Once again, Danny tried to catch Michelle's eye, but she was frozen in place and wouldn't look at him. Danny figured she felt humiliated, too.

Once the reception hall was clear, Nemathes closed the doors. He moved warily to the king. "You surprised me, Sire," he said. "When I suggested that you give a counteroffer, I had no idea …"

"What choice did I have?" the king answered peevishly.

"None, of course," Nemathes replied.

Stefan looked at Michelle, but she kept her gaze down. "You don't agree," he guessed.

"I'm not allowed to argue with you," Michelle said evasively. "You're the king."

"Don't you forget it," Stefan said sternly. "And as the king, I must think of the welfare of my people before my own pride. You are a child and cannot possibly understand."

"I understand that you gave in."

The king sat up and poked a finger in her direction. "Not that I ever have to explain myself, but I want you to be educated in the ways of leadership. Because Fendar cursed our money, we have been relying on our lumber trade as a means of barter with the other nations. To lose that would ruin us financially. We would be a bankrupt nation."

"So Fendar has won."

"He hasn't won," the king said, a sly smile forming on his lips. "I said they could go. But I didn't say *when* they could go."

Nemathes was instantly concerned. "Sire, you don't mean to renege on your promise," he said anxiously.

The king shook his head, but the smile stayed. "I will not renege. I will simply *postpone*."

Michelle giggled and wondered what Danny would say to that.

Fendar and Wondrar met with the Marutian elders to discuss how to get the thousands of people out of the city without a lot of confusion and chaos. Now that freedom from Muirk was a distinct possibility, even for a few days, the elders were hopeful.

A feeling of celebration seemed to move throughout the Promised Land. Danny noticed that the people on the street were smiling more. Even those Marutians who had been beaten and sent out to the mines and fields for more than 12 hours that day reacted happily to the news.

Privately, Fendar told Danny, "Once they have a taste of

freedom, they'll want more. These days out will stir them. You watch and see."

That evening, Fendar and Wondrar continued to discuss plans for evacuating the Marutians. They pored over maps and debated routes and bickered over details like the two brothers they were. Danny and Wayne, who learned to play a Marutian board game involving cards and pegs, watched them with amusement.

"Does this mean we're going back to Odyssey now?" Wayne asked while Danny drew a card and then moved a peg three squares on the board.

"I don't know," Danny replied. "If this is what we came to do, I guess we can go home."

"But I haven't done my part," Wayne said. "Remember? One of us is supposed to raise a cloud or something like that."

"Maybe you'll do it when we all go out to the forest."

"I think they're smoke signals," Wayne said as he took his turn at the game.

"What?"

"Like Indians," he explained. "I'll bet there'll be a big bonfire in the forest, and I'll be in charge of sending smoke signals."

Danny rolled his eyes. "You're goofy."

"What other kind of cloud goes up?" he asked.

Just then they heard a knock at the door, and Wondrar answered it. Jakin, the leader of the small band of Marutian rebels, came in. His face was overcast with bad news.

"What's wrong?" Fendar asked immediately.

"My spies at the palace have brought me some disturbing news," Jakin reported. He sat down at the table and poured himself a drink of water. After he drank it, he said, "Everyone at court is laughing at us."

Fendar sat down next to him. "Why are they laughing?"

"Because the word has gone around that the king has no intention of allowing us to leave."

"He gave his word that we could."

"But he didn't say *when* we could. My spies tell me that he will wait until the idea of leaving is forgotten or—" Jakin paused for a moment.

"Or?"

"Or until the time is right to arrest you and try you for murder."

Fendar's cheeks turned red. He clenched his hand into a fist and brought it down on the table. Cups and bowls rattled, and crumbs of bread scattered. But he said nothing.

"Does anyone else know about this?" Wondrar asked.

Jakin shook his head, but his face was bright. "I came to you first. This is just the sort of thing my rebels need to get the people motivated. When they catch the king in a bold-faced lie—"

"Or this news will deflate the people's hopes," Wondrar said with a frown. "The people will play into the king's hands and forget about freedom." He looked at his brother. "And if he continues to work them as hard as he has, you will be seen as their true enemy. They won't fight for freedom but instead will happily hand you over for execution."

"Do you think so poorly of our kinsmen?" Jakin asked as a rebuke of Wondrar.

"Yes, I do. We are a fickle lot. We have exchanged our freedom for comfort and security. We have ignored the Unseen One. We have sold our souls to the Palatians."

Fendar suddenly stood up and exclaimed, "Then we will not play the king's waiting game. I will put it to him *tonight* to say when we may go. If he evades the question, he will have to answer to the Unseen One."

Michelle was enjoying the evening with King Stefan, his wife, Chardan, and their two sons, Penthan and Rathan. Michelle hadn't even realized that King Stefan was married until he invited her to dinner in the royal apartments. Nemathes explained that Stefan kept his family away from the politics of the land. Except for state occasions when the entire family had to be present, they lived privately and secluded from royal demands. Nemathes said, "When the time comes, King Stefan will train his firstborn son for his role as the future king. But right now, the boy is only five. The king wants him to enjoy his childhood while he can."

Dinner was a lavish affair held in the king's private dining room. Though he said it was an informal occasion, he made sure his servants were dressed to the hilt and served a six-course meal that included various kinds of meats, fruits, vegetables, and sweet puddings at the end. Chardan, who refused to be called a queen, chatted amiably with Michelle, asking all kinds of questions about Odyssey. She was a kind woman with a round, friendly face and curly, brown hair that she tied up in a bun.

Penthan and Rathan, who favored their father's looks, sat quietly and politely during the meal. Afterward, they made up for lost time by exhausting Michelle with stories and games.

Michelle was overwhelmed with feelings she hadn't experienced in a long time. She was part of a family. Her parents had divorced a long time ago, and, apart from being shuttled back and forth between them, the only other family she had was when she visited Danny and Wayne. She never enjoyed that much, mostly because she was jealous of their life together. But tonight, here in Muirk with the king and queen and the two young princes, she felt like a member of their family. The king listened to her. The queen was interested in what she had to say. The young boys liked her. She had a special place here, a place she didn't have with her busy mother or her remarried father. She *belonged*.

Late in the evening. when Michelle began to think it was time to go back to her room, Nemathes came to the door. He spoke quietly to the king and then left. Stefan apologized to his wife and asked Michelle to come with him.

"Is something wrong?" Michelle asked as they left the apartments and walked down the hallway to the front of the palace.

"Our friends have returned," Stefan said.

"So late?"

The king snorted. "Marutians are not known for their manners. Normally I wouldn't meet anyone at this hour, but Nemathes advises that I should. And, as you know, I do everything Nemathes tells me to do."

The king and Michelle laughed together as they entered the reception hall. Fendar, Wondrar, Danny, and Wayne stood in the center of the room. Michelle searched their faces to see what they might be up to, but she couldn't detect anything in their solemn expressions.

"Consider yourselves honored," the king said as he took his throne. "Now, what's so important that I interrupted my time with my family and a guest to meet with you?"

"A question of integrity," Fendar announced. His voice was low and full of anger.

"Whose integrity?"

"Yours."

The king looked at Nemathes. "Is this fugitive questioning the integrity of the king?" he asked.

"It sounds as if he is," Nemathes replied.

Fendar feigned politeness. "I'm certain that it is a misunderstanding on my part. Your Highness said earlier today that the Marutians could go out of Muirk to worship the Unseen One. May I ask *when* we may go?"

"I'll let you know," the king said casually.

"It would be best for all if you said so *now*." Fendar's eyes seemed to burn into the king. "There are so many plans to be made, you see."

The king considered Fendar, then said, "At an appropriate time."

"When?" Fendar asked more firmly.

Sitting up in his throne, Stefan lost the casual tone in his voice. "When I say so."

"You're toying with us."

"I am your king. You don't dare accuse me of anything," Stefan hissed.

"Ah, but I *do* accuse you, Sire. You have no intention of allowing us to leave Muirk—not now, not later."

The king stood up. "I should have locked you up the first moment you set foot in Muirk!"

"You have no authority over me," Fendar said, his voice a low growl. "Danny."

As Danny stepped forward, the king said derisively, "The glory of Palatia will fade before my very eyes. Yes, yes, I've heard it before."

Danny blushed slightly, then stammered, "Eat as much as you can tonight. Tomorrow your plates will be empty."

Wondrar took the walking stick with both hands and moved it in a large circle. Then he walked out.

Fendar remained long enough to add, "The choice was yours from the beginning. You could have acknowledged the

Unseen One. But your stubbornness has made you blind, and Palatia will now suffer as it has never suffered before." Fendar then left with Danny and Wayne trailing behind.

"What can he do to us?" Stefan asked Nemathes. "There must be a limit to their power."

"Perhaps," a pale and worried Nemathes answered. "And perhaps their limits are beyond our endurance."

"Is anything beyond my endurance?" King Stefan gibed his adviser.

"We shall see," Nemathes responded.

Michelle thought she'd never heard a voice so full of gloom.

That night, while the Palatians slept, a white mist drifted through their fields of wheat and corn, their gardens of vegetables, and their orchards. As the mist passed, the plants and trees withered and died.

In other fields and pastures, cattle and sheep, chickens and pigs all stirred restlessly as if they sensed the coming catastrophe. Then each in its turn breathed its last breath and collapsed where it was. By morning, the corpses were rotten and inedible.

Unable to sleep, Michelle stood at her bedroom window and saw the moving mist without knowing what it meant. Her mind was already pondering the day ahead. *The king has to stay firm,* she thought. *If he gives in to Fendar, I'll have to go back to face Danny and Wayne. Then we would probably go back to our own world. And right now, that's the last place I want to be.*

CHAPTER ELEVEN

───────◆───────

The next day, King Stefan's soldiers raided the Promised Land. The crops and animals there hadn't died the night before, and the soldiers thought they could take the food into Muirk. But the instant their wagons reached the gate, the crops withered and the animals died. In retaliation, Marutian workers were taken to the fields of dead crops and animals and forced to burn or bury them.

Regmund and the elders cornered Fendar and Wondrar at the apartment. "King Stefan wants our men to work until they drop!" Regmund complained. "Our people are beaten without reason."

"So they are finally being treated as the slaves they truly are," Fendar observed. "Maybe now they will long for their true home in Marus."

One of the other elders said accusingly, "That's easy for you to say! You don't feel the lash of the whip on your back! You haven't been clubbed until you were half dead!"

"Perhaps you'd be happier if I turned myself over to the king and allowed him to execute me?" Fendar challenged them. "Is that what you want—to go back to how things have been? Do you care so little for the Unseen One and His desire for you?"

"We didn't expect this kind of trouble," Regmund admitted.

"The Unseen One has spared you from all the pain He has poured out on the Palatians. Yet He is still too much trouble for you?"

Regmund shuffled uneasily. "What good does it do us if the king won't let us go?"

"He *will* let us go," Fendar said firmly. "But it may take time. Watch and see the wonders the Unseen One will perform."

Fendar, Wondrar, Danny, and Wayne went directly to the palace. This time Nemathes met them at the gate. Danny wondered what had become of Michelle.

"The king will not see you today," announced Nemathes. Danny thought the king's magician looked older somehow.

"Then his heart is still unmoved?" Fendar confirmed.

"It is."

Fendar sighed deeply and gestured to Danny.

"The glory of Palatia will fade before your eyes," he said.

With both hands, Wondrar held the walking stick up over his head. "Palatia's great warships, the envy of the world, will disappear. Tell your king that the Unseen One is far greater."

"With a wave of your stick, you think you can obliterate the might of the Palatian navy?" Nemathes seemed to ask more out of curiosity than disbelief.

"Until the king relents, you will see this—and much worse," Fendar replied.

King Stefan's meeting with his military advisers had turned into a shouting match. Michelle watched silently from her chair near the door. Only when the king brought his fist down onto the table did the assembly quiet enough to hear him.

"I never expected to see my generals and admirals in such a childish panic," the king said scornfully. "Speak to me, Admiral Altec."

"The entire fleet has sunk, Your Highness," reported a stiff-gated man in a deep blue coat with epaulets on the shoulders. "We were fortunate to rescue all of the ships' crews, with only a handful of minor injuries."

"How did it happen?" the king asked.

"The hulls on the ships simply fractured and burst. The ships sank faster than anything our most experienced commanders have ever seen."

"Was it sabotage?"

"Sabotage!" the admiral cried out. "Sire, these doings are not manmade. They are of supernatural origin. Surely you must know that! Even in the coastal towns, we know of Fendar and his powers."

"Then we have our work cut out for us. We must rebuild the fleet."

The admiral shook his head and said mournfully, "It will take months, years! And in the meantime, we are laid open to our enemies along the seafront."

"We are laid open to worse things than that if I give in to Fendar!" the king snapped.

One of the generals stood up. "Worse, Sire?" he asked. "What could be worse than this?"

The king leveled a harsh gaze at him. "You have lived too long in leisure—you have become soft—if you think it cannot be worse. Consider our enemies attacking us from all sides. That is what they will surely do if I allow Fendar and his Marutians to leave. This is a battle of endurance. If we lose to Fendar, what message does that send to the other kings? They will consider me a weak monarch, one who will be easily conquered. We'll have no end of attacks after that. So be strong, be resolved! We *must* win against Fendar."

"How will you win against him?" the admiral inquired.

"His powers seem to protect him. And your wizards are use-less," he added sarcastically, gesturing to Nemathes.

Michelle looked over at Nemathes, who, admittedly, looked pale and tired. She imagined that he was staying up nights trying to find a way to fight Fendar with magic.

King Stefan rose to his full height and said, "I will come down on the Marutians with an iron fist!" To accent the point, he brought his own fist down on the table.

This worried Michelle. She imagined that he would begin to hurt the Marutians, which didn't fit into the game she had in mind. After the assembly had been dismissed, she asked the king what he meant by his words.

"I will work them harder, that's all," he assured her. "Unlike Fendar, I am not a killer."

But Michelle couldn't see what Danny and Wayne witnessed first-hand. The king's army was given free rein to do what it liked with the people of Marus. At first the soldiers simply beat and abused the workers. Then they marched through the streets of the Promised Land and lashed out at anyone who got in their way.

"It's a show of power," Wondrar said as they watched from the apartment window.

Jakin and a small group of rebels skirmished with some of the soldiers in the back streets, but they were driven off with muskets and swords.

"Are we going to stand by and let this happen?" Wondrar asked his brother.

"We must follow the plan laid out for us by the Unseen One," Fendar replied. "We will go to the king again and give him the chance to change his mind."

So the four of them returned to the palace that evening. Nemathes greeted them at the gate once again—before they even got out of the wagon—with a message from the king. "His Highness doesn't want to be interrupted," he informed them. "He is having supper with his family and Michelle, his ward."

"His *ward?*" Wayne asked. "Does that mean she's like a princess or something?"

"Or something," Nemathes replied dryly.

Fendar was adamant. "I believe he'll want to see us now. Otherwise he'll regret the consequences."

"Your threats are lost on him," Nemathes said.

"Then please pass on a message from us."

Nemathes watched impatiently, with his arms folded, while Danny said, "The glory of Palatia will fade before your eyes."

"Be warned tonight that, by the power of the Unseen One, tomorrow will bring destruction," added Fendar. "The great buildings of Palatia—the palaces, temples, arenas, and museums—will all crumble. Even Muirkostle will fall. Evacuate them or lives will be lost."

Nemathes, who had looked pale before, now went completely white. "I . . . will inform His Highness," he stammered.

Fendar stepped closer to Nemathes. "In case he is tempted to think this is an idle threat," Fendar warned, "tell him to travel to the mausoleum in the royal park. There he will receive a foretaste of what will come unless he changes his mind."

Nemathes bowed. "I will tell him."

Nemathes watched as Wondrar turned the wagon around and drove it back onto the boulevard in front of the palace. It disappeared from his view. Gathering his robe up, he raced back to the palace and straight to the king's private chambers.

The king was having his evening meal with his family and Michelle. He looked annoyed to have been interrupted until Nemathes explained what Fendar had said.

Losing no time, the king called for his royal carriage to be brought to the front of the palace. He wanted to see for himself what had happened to his family's mausoleum. Michelle, who was disappointed to have their family time undone by bad news, went with the king and Nemathes.

The royal park was dark except for an occasional street lamp that lit the main drive to and around the lake. Michelle hadn't been to this park before, so she didn't know what to expect. To her, the black patches of trees and the reflection of the night sky shimmering on the lake made it look like any other park she'd seen—except for the two moons, of course.

The king suddenly gasped "No!" and pounded on the roof of the carriage for the driver to stop. The horses snorted and the carriage lurched as the king leaped out the door. Nemathes was right behind him. Confused, Michelle followed.

A path led up to broad, stone steps. At the top of the steps was a mound of rubble, as if an earthquake had shaken down whatever building was there. Michelle could barely make out the arches and pillars that lay haphazardly on the heap.

The king stood at the bottom of the steps, his face a rigid mask of fury. Nemathes watched his sovereign carefully, unsure what might happen next.

"My parents are in there," the king finally said, a quiver in his voice. "How does he dare such profanity? I curse the day he was born!"

"Sire, he swears that all the great buildings of Palatia will fall, exactly like this one," Nemathes reminded him.

The king was silent for a moment, then slowly sat down on the step. "We cannot let him," he said simply.

"How will we stop him?"

"How else? We must let the Marutians go."

"Does Your Highness mean it this time? They will not tolerate any tricks."

"I have just said so, haven't I?" Stefan said angrily. He looked up at Michelle, who stood by without knowing what to say. "You are disappointed in me, I know. But unless you give me power like Fendar's or wisdom I cannot find for myself, I must concede. I can't bear to sit idly by and watch the destruction of our city."

Michelle shook her head. "I'm sorry, Sire."

"We must inform them immediately. This curse will come before morning otherwise."

The king stood up. "Take the carriage to their district and tell them of my decision," he ordered Nemathes. "But tell them also that I want them to leave in the morning. Not the day after or the next week or the next month. If they want time to go into the wilderness to worship, let them go immediately. Go— and take their curses with them!"

"How will you return to the palace?" Nemathes asked.

"My ward and I will walk."

With a quick bow, Nemathes strode off to the carriage. A moment later, the driver shouted at the horses and the carriage rattled off.

King Stefan and Michelle began their walk back to the palace. Michelle had thought that the king wanted to talk to her, but he didn't say a word. He seemed lost in his thoughts. Michelle decided it was probably just as well. She didn't have anything encouraging to offer. In fact, if she spoke, she would have told him that he had done the right thing. As much as she hated to admit it—and she knew she couldn't bear to face Danny and Wayne after this—Fendar had them beaten.

It took them nearly half an hour to get back to the palace. Michelle wasn't sure what time it was now, but it seemed late. She felt tired from the walk. As they entered through the front doors, Chardan approached with the two princes. The boys rushed to their father's arms.

"They refused to go to bed until they knew you were all right," Chardan explained. "Somehow they got the idea that if the family mausoleum fell, our whole family would collapse."

Stefan knelt down, pulled his sons onto his knees, and said softly, "No, my sons. You are safe."

"Did you make the bad man go away?" Penthan asked.

The king looked at him somberly. "The bad man will leave us alone now, I think."

"You are giving Fendar what he wants?" Chardan asked, surprised.

"Yes. The Marutians can go worship their god for a few days."

"Oh." Chardan's tone caused Michelle to look up at her. Her face betrayed her disappointment.

Stefan noted it, too, and pondered her quizzically. "Is something wrong?" he asked.

"No," Chardan said, but obviously something *was* wrong. "It's only that I've been telling your sons how you are the king and would never give in to the demands of mere slaves."

Stefan's cheeks turned red. "I am not giving in," he countered. "I am merely making a small concession."

"If you say so." Chardan beckoned the children to come to her.

"Chardan!"

She looked at her husband uncomfortably. "We shouldn't talk about this in front of the children or our guest."

"We can certainly talk about it now," the king said angrily, standing up fully again. "What do you mean?"

"Must I spell it out? You have been defeated by your former brother, and now I must think of a way to explain it so they'll understand." She turned to the two boys, who watched their parents with confused expressions, and said, "Come to bed now." Then she led them down the hall and back to their chambers.

"Do you agree with her?" Stefan asked Michelle.

"You've done the smart thing," Michelle said. "You had to give in to Fendar or everything would've fallen down."

"You use the same phrase: 'give in.' So that's how you see it, too. Fendar has defeated me."

Michelle stammered, "He hasn't *defeated* you. You wouldn't still be king if he defeated you. It's like you said. You made a concession."

"Words," he growled. "Meaningless words. I'm sick of them." As he stormed off, he shouted like a little boy, "I'll show you! I'll show all of you!"

Uh-oh, Michelle thought. *I didn't handle that well at all.*

CHAPTER TWELVE

As the sun came up, Danny and Wayne stood out in the chilly morning air, watching with amazement as wagons were loaded quickly for the trip out of Muirk. Ever since Nemathes had come the night before to deliver the news, the Marutians had been abuzz with excitement. For many, it would be the first time they'd ever left the confines of Muirk. Candles and lamps had burned all night as food was made and provisions were assembled. Thousands of men, women, and children worked like bees to get packed. Fendar and Wondrar coordinated with Regmund and the elders to make their departure as quick and smooth as possible. Danny knew that, in the backs of their minds, they half expected the king to double-cross them again.

Shortly after the sun had cleared the horizon, Danny stood with Wayne, Fendar, and Wondrar at the gate separating the Promised Land from Muirk. They were only moments from the mass exodus into the country. Once again, Danny wondered what this meant for him, Wayne, and Michelle. Would they be able to go back to Odyssey now?

An odd sound distracted Danny from the final efforts to leave. It reminded him of a crackling fire, but it was far too loud for that. Then he realized it was the sound of marching feet—hundreds of marching feet. Danny stood up on a wagon and looked from the gate in the direction of the city center. Through the scattered buildings and trees, he could see a long line of gray and an intermittent flashing as the sun caught polished metal. *A parade?* he wondered. Was it possible the king was having a celebratory parade? Or maybe it was an official escort.

Some of the Marutians also heard the sound and pointed in that direction.

"Soldiers!" Wayne exclaimed.

Fendar and Wondrar had taken notice now.

Snakelike, a formation of soldiers rounded a corner and headed for the gate. Some stationed themselves directly in front of the gate, while others continued straight past and took up positions along the outside of the wall surrounding the Marutian district. The Marutians grew silent.

The officer in charge came forward. "You are Fendar?" he asked Fendar.

"You know I am, Colonel Lanse," Fendar said to the man.

They obviously knew each other from Fendar's past life, which embarrassed the officer. He blushed and continued, "By order of the king, I am putting a stop to this illegal assembly and arresting you for treason."

Fendar laughed. "You're joking," he said dismissively.

"I'm afraid not. You are to come with me." The colonel stepped forward to take Fendar's arm.

Jakin suddenly broke through the crowd with a knife in hand. "Let him go, you treacherous—" he shouted.

Fendar grabbed Jakin's hand as the line of soldiers lifted their muskets to shoot him. "Stop, Jakin!" Fendar ordered. "This is not the way."

"You won't let them take you. The king will kill you without a trial," Jakin warned.

"Don't worry about me. Worry about getting the Marutians safely back into their houses."

Jakin looked puzzled.

Another sign was coming, Danny felt. It had appeared in

his mind's eye like a clear picture, only it was a picture that didn't make sense to him. He saw all of Muirk buried in a terrible blizzard. But how could that be? It was summertime.

Fendar approached Colonel Lanse and told him, "Colonel, I suggest you return to the king and tell him that the Unseen One will not be mocked. He has had several chances now to do the right thing. Must he suffer yet another sign to demonstrate the Unseen One's power?"

Colonel Lanse looked bored. "You can tell him yourself, Fendar," he replied. "Come along quietly."

"But it's not for me to go with you. I will meet the king on the Unseen One's terms, not his."

"Yes, yes, now let's go." He reached out for Fendar.

Wondrar stepped between the two men, the walking stick held firm in front of him.

"No tricks now," Lanse said. "My men are ordered to shoot to kill."

"How can they kill what they cannot see?" Wondrar asked. He brought the bottom of the stick down onto the ground with a loud rap. The soldiers cried out, dropped their rifles, and covered their eyes.

Colonel Lanse, who was unaffected by whatever had happened, turned to his men and shouted, "What's wrong with you?"

No sooner were the words out of his mouth than a harsh, cold wind began to blow. It came at gale force and buffeted the soldiers, sending their rifles flying away. They stumbled out of control against the wind.

To everyone's astonishment, snow began to fall. It wasn't the gentle, Christmassy kind but the awful, horizontal kind that sticks to everything and gathers faster than you can shovel it. In a matter of seconds, the ground was covered.

Danny now did a double take, looking at the soldiers in

Muirk, then back at the Marutians who stood behind the gate to the Promised Land, and then at the soldiers again. It was still a sunny, calm day in the district. But the blizzard Danny had imagined was now hitting with full force on the other side of the gate. The soldiers scattered in all directions, as if they'd been blown like dead leaves.

Colonel Lanse didn't seem to know what to do now. No one had anticipated this in his orders. "Fendar, stop it!" he finally ordered.

"Take the message to your king," Fendar said. "All Palatia will be covered in snow and ice. I will be pleased to meet him when he wishes to talk."

Colonel Lanse closed his eyes as if wishing he were somewhere else entirely. Resigned, he turned and made his way into the blizzard.

Fendar climbed onto the wagon and shouted at the Marutians, "Remember what you see here! Remember how you are favored by the Unseen One!"

Danny looked through the gate, as if through a window, at the raging storm beyond.

As soon as Morgon woke her up to see the snow, Michelle knew what had happened. The king had changed his mind, and Fendar had called down another sign. By the time she'd dressed and gone to the king's council chambers, the snow was several feet deep, with drifts even higher. The servants couldn't get the front doors of the palace open at all.

Michelle had no idea how the king had managed to get his advisers assembled, but they were all together in the council chambers with the king and Nemathes.

Nemathes, looking more strained and anxious than ever, was speaking as Michelle slipped in through the door. "You must relent," he was saying. "While your power as an earthly king is unquestioned and greater than any in the world, you are battling supernatural forces."

"Has my chief adviser become a coward?" the king asked.

"My courage is not the question here, Sire," Nemathes replied, stung but adamantly diplomatic. "I am your chief adviser in order to bring wisdom and understanding to this council. I would be disloyal not to speak the truth."

"What do the rest of you say?" the king demanded.

Penwyth, the older gentleman Michelle had seen in another council meeting, cleared his throat and said, "This freak snowstorm will cripple the nation. No one can travel in it. Our army is immobilized. Our trade routes are cut off. When you consider the effects of Fendar's other tricks on our money and our food supplies, we will be in dire straits in no time at all."

"What are you suggesting?"

"Only what I have always suggested: Find a way to compromise with the fiend."

"How?"

"Tell him that only the Marutian *men* may go to worship the Unseen One. With their women and children stuck here, they'll have to stay on their best behavior."

"And if he refuses?"

All the advisers averted their gazes from the king.

"I see. If he refuses, you'll expect me to give in to Fendar completely."

"You had the opportunity last night," Nemathes reminded him.

Stefan glared at his chief counselor. "I had very good reasons for changing my mind."

Michelle knew what those reasons were, and she wondered if anyone else in the room would agree that they were good.

"All right," the king finally agreed. "I will send a messenger to tell Fendar I'll meet with him. But I'll wait until he arrives before I present any details. And I'll only meet with him if he gets rid of the snow first."

"He'll have to get rid of the snow if he hopes to come to the palace," Penwyth joked.

The advisers agreed that this was a good way to proceed, and the king called for a messenger to go to the Marutian district.

It took the poor messenger a long time to travel across the city to the Marutian district. The wind and snow gave even the strongest of horses a nearly impossible task. The morning became afternoon, and then, to everyone's surprise, the wind died down and the snow stopped falling. Soon the summer sun broke through the clouds.

"I assume he finally got the message," the king said as he watched from one of the reception hall windows. When he was sure the snow was truly melting, he called for Colonel Lanse to come see him. Nemathes and Michelle exchanged uneasy looks. Why did he want the colonel? Did the king have another plan he wasn't sharing with them?

The king spoke softly to the colonel so that no one else could hear what he was saying. The colonel saluted, said, "Yes, Your Highness," and left.

"Your Highness?" Nemathes asked.

The king waved him away. "I'm simply taking a precaution," he said dismissively.

Fendar, Wondrar, Danny, and Wayne arrived much later that afternoon. They stood before King Stefan in the reception hall. Michelle, Nemathes, and the other advisers stood nearby to witness the encounter.

Fendar said, "In good faith, the Unseen One has brought back the sun. Will you now let us go?"

The king, who sat on his throne, responded quickly, "Tell me first whom you plan to take along with you."

"All the Marutians, of course," Fendar replied, puzzled.

"Ah," Stefan said, as if this were a revelation to him, "I didn't realize you had hoped to take everyone with you."

"What trick is this?" Wondrar fumed.

"I have assumed all along that you wanted to take the Marutian *men* only," the king said innocently.

"We are taking *everyone*, Sire," Fendar insisted.

The king shook his head sadly. "I'm afraid that you can't. You may take the men, but you must leave the women and children behind."

Fendar stood his ground. "*All* of us must go, Sire."

The king spread his hands helplessly. "But if all of you go, how will I know you'll come back?"

"You have my word as a voice of the Unseen One."

"You swear upon something that means nothing to me!" Stefan snapped. "It's not good enough."

"Then by your own word do you bring judgment against your nation," warned Fendar.

"And you bring suffering to your own," the king retorted. "Even while we speak, my soldiers are descending upon the Marutians. I will fill my dungeons and prisons with as many of you as I can!"

The assembled crowd gasped with surprise. *So that's why the king wanted to speak with Colonel Lanse,* Michelle thought.

She glanced over at Danny and Wayne. They looked shocked. Danny caught her eye and shook his head. She'd never seen him look so sad. She wondered if he felt sad because the king had double-crossed them again or for some other reason. What would Fendar do now?

She suddenly felt sick in the pit of her stomach. They were no longer dealing with disappearing money, rotten clothing, or skin problems. The thought of people jammed into dungeons wasn't what she had in mind. This wasn't merely a contest of wills anymore. She wished it would stop. This was getting far too serious.

"Do you think I'm a fool?" the king shouted at Fendar. "I know what you're doing. You want to take your people out of Muirk for a few days so they'll realize what freedom is like. Once you've done that, there'll be no living with them. I'll be dealing with every rebel and revolutionary in your district."

Fendar was unperturbed. His voice, low and commanding, rattled the windows. "Save yourself—and your people—by allowing the Marutians to return to their land *now*."

"Never!"

"So be it," Fendar said, sounding to Michelle like the voice of doom.

Danny suddenly spoke up. "Long ago, Marus was called to be a light to the nations," he began. "Its light will expose everything for what it truly is."

Before Michelle realized what was happening, Wondrar lifted and threw the walking stick down. It stabbed into the floor like a spear, shattering the marble and tiles. He let go of it, and it stood upright and still. The crowd stepped back, fearful of what it might do.

The handle of the walking stick began to glow a dull red, a pinkish color, and then white. The whiteness of the light grew and then fanned out sheetlike to the rest of the room. It got brighter and brighter until the natural shadows of the room grew long and then snapped like rubber bands into oblivion.

"What are you doing?" King Stefan called out as he tried unsuccessfully to protect his eyes. The light seemed to penetrate through his hands.

"A plague of light," Fendar said, then motioned for Wondrar and the two boys to follow him. To everyone's amazement, they left the walking stick in the floor of the reception room. The king drew a sword from a sheath that had hung on the wall and raced to strike down the walking stick. No matter how many times he struck, however, the stick didn't move, nor was it even scratched by the blade.

Michelle turned her head against the wall and tried to block out the light, but it was impossible. The light was relentless. It penetrated and illuminated everything. She couldn't even close her eyes and hope for darkness.

I thought I was immune, she thought. But this time she wasn't. The light tore into her. She wondered how long someone could endure such a light before going mad.

CHAPTER THIRTEEN

———◆———◆———

The light in the Promised Land was as normal as it could be. The sun faded into the evening, and then night came. Muirk, on the other hand, glowed so brightly that even when all the curtains were drawn, extra blankets were added to the windows, and pillows were piled on their heads, people still couldn't sleep. Occasionally, a Palatian came to the gates and screamed at the Marutians in wild profanities. Other Palatians simply screamed from the pain caused by the light.

Danny lay awake for the longest time, wondering how Michelle was coping. Was she able to escape the endless light? Her expression, when Wondrar had jammed the walking stick into the floor, made Danny think she hadn't escaped it. She must have been suffering whatever the rest of the Palatians suffered. He found himself praying that Michelle would be all right.

Back at Muirkostle, Michelle prayed the exact same thing for herself. Whether her eyes were open or closed, it didn't matter—the light came through. If she put her head under a pillow, crawled under the bed, or hid in the wardrobe, the light still came through. She imagined the deepest, darkest cellar in Palatia was ablaze with this light.

No one in the palace could sleep any better than the rest of the Muirkians. Michelle suspected that no one in all of Palatia could sleep, either. The light went on.

The next day, the king brought in all his advisers, military personnel, and magicians to try to destroy the walking stick and stop the light. But no amount of pulling with ropes or attacks with swords or axes affected the stick. It stood in the ground as if it had always been there and always would be.

On the second day, the king showed no signs of relenting to Fendar. Michelle, her head aching from the light and lack of sleep, spent the day doing nothing. She wandered around the palace like a small ghost. She eventually went to the king's chambers to make sure Chardan and the children were all right.

Chardan came to the door, looking pale and exhausted, and frowned at Michelle. "My children have been crying all night," she reported, as if it were Michelle's fault.

"I'm sorry. Is there anything I can do?" Michelle asked.

"You can go back to wherever you came from," Chardan told her in a cold voice.

The statement stung Michelle. "What do you mean?"

"I had hoped that by allowing you to be a part of our family, you might persuade Fendar to give up. But you haven't. You haven't done a thing since you arrived here. My husband thinks you're something special, but as far as I can see, you are part of our troubles. So why don't you go away?" Chardan then slammed the door in Michelle's face.

For the rest of that day and into the night, Michelle wept as she had never wept before. In that endless light, the tears seemed to sparkle like jewels as they fell.

I've been rejected again, she thought. *No matter where I go or what I try to do, I'm not accepted. No family will have me—not my own, not the king's, not even Danny and Wayne's.* In the deepest part of her pity, she wondered if she would ever find a place to belong, a home for herself.

When she thought she could cry no more, she lay in bed and stared at the insides of her bright eyelids until she lost track of time.

The third day came with the sound of a commotion on the

palace lawns. People were gathering, many as protesters. They shouted their demand for the king to put an end to their troubles. They had suffered enough, they said. Michelle watched as Stefan's guards went out to disperse the crowd. But the guards were outnumbered and ultimately had to retreat into the palace. Morgon arrived and said there was going to be a gathering in the king's council chambers.

Still exhausted, Michelle got up, dressed, and went to the meeting. Stefan's advisers had already arrived. They whispered among themselves, wondering what the king would do. Nemathes entered, looking frightful and sick. Michelle had no doubt that he had spent all this time trying to overcome the powers of the Unseen One. But there was no overcoming *this*, Michelle knew.

After nearly an hour of waiting, the king finally came in. He looked like a mess. His hair was disheveled, and his eyes were wild. Something about his demeanor made him seem more unpredictable than ever. Nemathes looked concerned. The advisers also exchanged worried glances. Michelle was hesitant to think it, but to her the king looked insane. Surely the endless light hadn't done that to him in only three days!

"I've summoned Fendar," Stefan said.

"What will you do, Sire?" Nemathes asked.

"Get him to turn off that blasted light, for a start."

Penwyth asked, "Will you allow the Marutians to go?"

King Stefan held up a finger. "You'll have to wait and see," he said.

Michelle wasn't comforted.

They adjourned to the reception hall as Fendar, Wondrar, Danny, and Wayne came in. Michelle thought the four of them looked healthier and stronger than ever. She imagined that the Marutian district was saved from the terrible light somehow.

King Stefan, positioned on his throne once more, waved at the walking stick. "We can't talk with that thing beaming at us," he said.

Wondrar went up to the stick and pulled it out of the floor. To everyone's relief, the light slowly faded. Michelle rubbed her eyes. Her headache began to fade. From outside, they could hear the people on the palace lawn applaud.

After a few minutes, when the light had returned to normal, the king said calmly to Fendar, "I've given due consideration to your request."

"And?" Fendar prompted.

"And I've decided that I will allow your people to go worship your god."

"*All* my people?"

"Yes."

Wondrar looked relieved. Wayne nudged Danny happily. But Danny didn't believe it was going to be so easy, and he could tell from Fendar's expression that he didn't believe it, either. Michelle was astounded.

Fendar said cautiously, "With all due respect, Sire, are there any conditions on your permission?"

"Conditions?" the king asked with that feigned innocent tone in his voice.

"We have come to this point too many times before," Fendar said candidly. "Are you saying that all Marutians are free to go out of the city to worship?"

"Yes. But—"

Danny braced himself.

The king continued, "I don't want you to take anything with you. Only the clothes on your backs and enough food for three days. You must leave all your possessions and valuables. That doesn't sound unreasonable, does it?"

Fendar scratched at his chin thoughtfully and then said, "I'm sorry, but that won't do."

"What do you mean?" the king asked impatiently. "I'm letting you go!"

"The Unseen One hasn't instructed me specifically about what our worship will be like. We may need some of our possessions with us."

"Which ones?"

"I won't know until we get there."

King Stefan could hardly contain his fury. "You expect me to allow you to leave with all your men, women, children, *and* possessions—and I'm supposed to believe you'll come back?"

"If I say we will come back, we will."

"How do I know that?"

"You will have to trust me, as I trust the Unseen One."

Stefan slammed his fists down on the armrests of his throne. "No!" he screamed. "I won't do it! I've conceded enough to you!"

Nemathes moved toward the throne, obviously to appeal to the king. Stefan pushed Nemathes away as he leaped to his feet and crossed the floor until he was only a foot from Fendar. He looked as if he might rain blows upon his former brother, but he kept his hands at his sides. He thrust his face toward Fendar and hissed, "Get out! Get out of my sight! You and your god can do what you will, but I swear to you, if I ever see your face again, you'll die!"

Fendar didn't move or flinch. He listened to the king with an unsettling serenity. When the king had clearly finished, Fendar replied, "It is true. I will never appear before you again."

He turned away from King Stefan and walked out of the reception hall. Still clasping the walking stick, Wondrar followed his brother. Wayne, clearly disappointed, shrugged and left. Danny remained, his gaze fixed on Michelle. He wanted her to come along. He *willed* her to.

"Oh, no," the king said in a half whisper to Danny. "She stays here with me. Maybe you should stay, too." He grabbed Danny's arm in a vicelike grip. Danny squirmed, but it was no use.

Suddenly Wondrar appeared in the doorway again. He stared at the king.

Stefan studied Wondrar, his eyes going from the man to the walking stick and back again. Then the king let go of Danny and stepped away. "It's no good without three children," he said as if he might burst out laughing. "You need three, and you've only got two."

Danny staggered back from the king and toward the door, rubbing his arm where the king had grabbed him. Wondrar put a hand on his shoulder and silently guided him out.

The king swung around to Nemathes, but he pointed to Michelle. "Make sure she's safely guarded," he ordered. "I don't want her to be tempted to join her friends."

"Sire!" Michelle cried out in protest.

He held his hand up. "Not a word, my dear. It's for the best. You'll see."

Nemathes asked, "But Sire, what happens now?"

"I intend to play this game to the death," the king replied resolutely.

The assembled council seemed to freeze at his words.

The king briskly rubbed his hands together. "I have been too lenient and understanding. It is a weakness of mine."

"What are you going to do?" Nemathes asked fearfully.

"I want every available soldier throughout the land to come to Muirk," said the king. "I will assemble a force so great and so powerful that the Marutians and their god will tremble to see it. Then I will burn the Marutian district to the ground. Let them live as slaves ought to live and see how they like it. They'll *beg* to be restored to my favor!"

"But Fendar's powers—"

"I don't care about his powers! The might of my army will strike so hard and so fast that he won't have time to conjure up any spells. Their onslaught will be final. By this time tomorrow, I will have control of my nation again!" The king swept out of the room like a wild whirlwind, taking his advisers with him.

Danny sat in the corner of the Marutian assembly room with Wayne, his heart in the grip of despair. In the moment when the king had grabbed his arm, he suddenly imagined what was going to happen next. In his mind, he saw terrible images of death and grief.

Meanwhile, around him, Fendar and Wondrar were listening to the complaints of Regmund and the rest of the Marutian elders. "The king will destroy us!" Regmund despaired.

"You've ruined everything!" another elder declared. "You took a good situation and turned it into a catastrophe!"

"Is your faith in the Unseen One so fragile?" Fendar asked them. "Haven't you seen enough of His power and glory to see that He will do what He says?"

"But *when?*" Regmund asked. "How many more signs must you throw at the king before he'll change his mind?"

Fendar shook his head in disappointment. "Don't you understand?" he asked, as if explaining something obvious to children. "The king wasn't supposed to change his mind until now."

"What?" the elders roared.

"The Unseen One wanted to demonstrate His power not only to the Palatians, but also to *you*. These signs were as much for *your* benefit as for the Palatians'. The Unseen One wanted you to see that He alone could safely lead you home again."

One of the elders stood up. "But the king will not see you again," he argued. "He said he'd kill you. What will the Unseen One do now?"

Fendar looked at the elders sadly. "He will now do the most difficult and painful thing that can be done. My brothers, prepare yourselves for the darkest of all nights."

Chapter Fourteen

◆━━━━━━━◆

The king was still in a defiant mood when the letter from Fendar arrived at the palace. He opened it and intended to read it in a mocking voice to his council. But the first words stopped him, and his tone became soft and extremely serious. The letter said:

> At midnight *tonight,* Death itself will pass through Palatia. *All the firstborn sons*—the heirs of Palatia's future—will be taken. From the oldest son of the king to the oldest son of the lowliest slave, no one will be spared. The cry of the Palatians will rise up like no cry *that has ever been heard before* or will be heard again. Then you *will* know that the Unseen One is the one true God over and above all. And *then* you will ask the Marutians to leave your country—not for *one day or two, but forever.*

The faces of the council members went pale. Their mouths hung open and their heads hung low.

Nemathes stared at the king. "You must let the Marutians go *now,*" he said.

King Stefan forced a disbelieving chuckle as he crumpled the letter. "This will not happen," he said confidently. "No one has this kind of power to pick and choose the victims of death. Not even Fendar." He turned to one of his generals. "When will our army be ready to invade the Marutian district?"

"First thing tomorrow," the general replied.

"If they want to see power, they'll see it then!" the king declared in a voice of bravado. The room replied with silence.

Michelle was locked in her room, and it wasn't until Morgon brought her lunch that she heard about Fendar's letter. "Everyone in the palace is talking about it," Morgon reported.

Michelle sat on the edge of her bed. She couldn't imagine that such a thing could possibly happen.

"You will not see me for the rest of the day," Morgon said as she put the tray of food on the end table. "I have a son. I am taking him away from Muirk until this has passed over."

Later that afternoon, Nemathes came to Michelle's room. "Come with me," he instructed.

"Where are we going?" she asked.

"We're going to find a way to stop Fendar."

In spite of the protests of the elders, Fendar persuaded the Marutians to pack their necessities into every available wagon and cart. "The king *will* allow us to leave," he assured them, "but we must go *immediately*. Bring only what you will need, not everything you want."

Most of the people were still in a state of disbelief. They had had so many close calls about leaving that they were doubtful about this one. But Fendar assured them repeatedly that the events to come would cause the king to relent.

That evening, Fendar gathered with Danny, Wayne, and all of Wondrar's family around the dining room table. In front of him was the chalice he'd brought from Gotthard, the one with the lamb's blood in it.

"This is our new beginning," Fendar announced as he put his hands on the chalice. "It is our Deliverance Day. Remember it well. Tell it to all the children of Marus in every generation to come." He took the cover off the chalice and dipped his thumb into the lamb's blood. Then he reached over to Maykar, Wondrar's oldest son, and rubbed the blood on his forehead. Up and down and side to side, he drew a *t*-shape. "All the firstborn who are sealed with this sign will not see Death tonight. And in years to come, it will become the seal of a promise, of Death's defeat for all who believe in the Unseen One."

After that, Wondrar went out into the Promised Land and called for all the firstborn children to come to his doorstep. When they arrived, Fendar and Wondrar dipped their thumbs into the chalice and gave the sign of the *t* to them all. Danny watched in wonder, because no matter how much blood the two men used from the chalice, it never ran out.

As the last of the children went past, Wayne suddenly nudged Danny. "Hey, you're the oldest," he said.

"So?"

"So you'd better get the sign or you might . . . you know."

Danny felt foolish. "I hadn't thought of that," he admitted. He went to Fendar and knelt down as the other firstborns had.

Fendar looked down at him. "You don't need this," he told Danny with a smile.

"I don't? Why not?" Danny asked.

"You already have the mark."

Surprised, Danny reached up to touch his forehead. "I do? But how? You haven't touched me with the blood yet."

Fendar shook his head. "It's not a mark on your forehead. You're somehow covered in the lamb's blood. The Unseen One must have sealed you in your world." Without further comment, Fendar turned away and went back inside Wondrar's house. Danny looked at Wayne.

Wayne shrugged. "What does it mean?" he asked.

"He must mean the mark of being a Christian," Danny suggested. "Didn't we learn something about that in Sunday school? It's because Jesus died on the cross."

Wayne nodded. "That must be it."

A moment later, Fendar returned to the doorstep with Wondrar and the walking stick. It was getting late. Danny knew that midnight was coming, and though he knew he was safe—knew it in the very core of his heart, far more than the scared-looking firstborn sons of Marus knew it—he dreaded what was about to happen.

In the center of the Promised Land was a large shopping square where merchants and tradesmen normally set up wagons of goods for sale. It was empty now. Fendar, Wondrar, and the two boys walked to the middle of the square.

"People of Marus!" Fendar called out. "Come now and pray to the Unseen One." His voice seemed to echo down every street and alleyway in the district. Slowly, the Marutians left their homes and crowded into the square. Wondrar found a wooden box for Fendar to stand on. He raised the walking stick and said, "Remember this night forever. When we arrive in Marus, as the Unseen One has promised, remember and celebrate this night. For you have been chosen by the Unseen One. You have been spared. Now bow your heads, one and all, and give thanks to our Deliverer."

The heads of the people bowed low. Fendar signaled Wondrar, Danny, and Wayne to come with him. They followed him away from the square and down the main street to the gate leading to Muirk. Somewhere in the distance, a clock began to strike for midnight.

"I hope this isn't my sign," Wayne whispered to Danny.

Danny agreed, his heart racing as they stopped at the gate and looked out on the quiet city. He felt a burning in his eyes and turned away from the others so as not to be seen crying.

Fendar put a hand on his shoulder. "We do well to weep," he said sadly. "There is no joy in what the Unseen One does now." Danny looked up at Fendar and saw that his eyes were filled with tears, too. So were Wondrar's. Even Wayne sniffed and lowered his head.

Wondrar took the walking stick and held it up to the city of Muirk. He didn't speak but slowly brought the stick down and touched it lightly to the ground.

Danny might have imagined it, but he thought he saw a small, inklike shadow trickle from the bottom of the stick and away into the city, growing and widening like a river. By the time the clock had chimed the twelfth note, Muirk seemed covered in darkness. Then the loud weeping and wailing began.

Michelle sat wearily watching Nemathes as he worked at his table in the dungeon. Throughout the evening, he had tried spells, incantations, elixirs, and potions, but he felt no confidence that any of them could protect the king's firstborn son. Then, just before midnight, he was overcome with despair and suddenly brushed his arms across the top of the table, pushing everything with a loud crash to the stony ground.

"The king will come and I'll have nothing for him!" Nemathes cried out. "What use am I?" Then he grabbed Michelle. "Do something!" he shouted at her. "You're from that world. You're supposed to be one of the signs. You must know how to protect us!"

Upset by Nemathes's outburst, Michelle cried, "I don't know what to do!"

The small, gold clock Nemathes kept on top of a wooden cabinet chimed for midnight. Nemathes looked at it wild-eyed and then struck it to the ground. He gazed at the shattered clock. "Oh, our foolish king!" he lamented. "If only he'd given Fendar what he wanted back in the beginning! If only he hadn't set his heart so stubbornly against the Marutian god!"

Nemathes spun toward Michelle again. She flinched as if he might strike out at her, too. Instead he went to a bookcase on the opposite wall behind her and poked and jabbed at the spines of the books there. "I have a collection of the Marutian legends," he said desperately. "Somewhere I'll find the meaning of this. I may not be able to stop what happens tonight, but I may be able to stop tomorrow. What does the legend say about the signs?"

While Nemathes pored over his books, Michelle quietly stood up and walked to the door. She wanted to go back to her room, get into her Odyssey clothes, and go away. She was no use to Nemathes. She was no good to the king. Why was she brought here at all?

Nemathes didn't seem to notice as she slipped out the door and climbed the cold, dark staircase back to the main level of the palace. She opened the door at the top and stepped into the hallway. Somewhere in the building, a woman wailed in a high, almost ghoulish cry. Michelle's skin crawled as she walked quickly toward her room. But she couldn't walk quickly enough. More shouts and cries came, echoing down the halls from all directions. A door slammed behind her and a sobbing man staggered past, his arms carrying a small bundle. Michelle pressed herself against the wall, too fearful to move. Nearby was an open window, and from the black expanse of the city came a chorus of lamentation. Michelle covered her ears and now ran and ran until she was buried under the pillows of her bed, but there was no escaping the grief.

Death had come, and Palatia would never be the same again.

The king summoned everyone in the palace to the reception room the next morning. Michelle, dressed in her Odyssey clothes, squeezed herself into the crowded room. The king had not bothered to put on his royal robes but stood before them in a plain, white shirt and dark trousers. His face was unshaven and his eyes were red-rimmed.

"Prince Penthan is dead," the king said simply.

Michelle felt a sob catch in her throat. She looked around for Nemathes, but he wasn't there.

"I know many others died last night," the king continued. "The god of Marus is a great and powerful god. He has crushed me under his heel." He lowered his head as if he couldn't say any more, but then he forced himself on. "I no longer care what becomes of the Marutians. Let them go. Let them take their god and leave us forever. I want no more to do with them."

So this is the end, Michelle thought. She wondered if she were now free to leave the palace. There was no point in staying any longer, she reasoned. If she could find Danny and Wayne, maybe they could all go back to their world together.

The king dismissed the assembly, and Michelle wanted to say good-bye, but the king had gone. It was probably just as well, she figured. If the king felt toward her as Chardan did, he wouldn't want to speak to her again anyway. She decided to go right then. Making her way to the front of the palace, she had just reached the ornate double doors when a voice called from behind her, "Stop!" It was Nemathes.

Michelle obeyed.

"Where do you think you're going?" he asked when he had caught up to her. He had the same wild-eyed look as he'd had before.

"I thought I would leave now," she explained.

He looked at her with a cruel expression. "Leave? Oh, but you can't. Not now."

"Then when?" she asked.

"You can't *ever* go," he declared. He grabbed her arm and dragged her back down the hall.

The Marutians gathered themselves into a long caravan of wagons, carts, and those on foot and waited by the gate for Fendar's signal. There was no doubt now that they would leave without interference. All of Jakin's spies had confirmed the king's words at the palace. Then, an hour later, a royal messenger had arrived with a message from the king. It was addressed to Regmund, not Fendar or Wondrar. The note said simply, "Go."

Regmund stood on a wagon and read it to all who could hear him. He then waved the letter, and a cry of celebration went up like the roar of a thousand lions. It was so loud that Danny and Wayne had to cover their ears.

Fendar was less jubilant. "We will celebrate when we reach Marus," he said. "We must leave Palatia now, while we can."

"The king isn't going to change his mind again, is he?" Wayne asked.

Fendar answered, "I won't predict what the king will or will not do. But we must seize the moment and leave."

"But what about Michelle?" Danny asked.

Fendar shook his head. "She is not coming with us."

Danny objected, "We can't leave her behind!"

"She is in the hands of the Unseen One."

Danny exchanged worried glances with Wayne, but they sat back on the wagon and hoped for the best.

Fendar nodded to Wondrar, who then gave a signal to the drivers of the first wagons to go. Slowly and clumsily, the caravan moved forward and through the gate. Many looked back upon the Promised Land with sadness. Others looked resolutely ahead. They followed a road that skirted the long way around the center of Muirk. Fendar had worried that the Palatians might attack or abuse them if they appeared to parade victoriously past them.

Even on the circuitous road, many Palatians came out to see the Marutians leave. Instead of abuse, the Palatians they met gave them provisions of food and fine blankets to take with them. Danny heard one old Palatian woman say, as she handed over bread and bottles of drink, "Go—before you kill us all!"

The entire population of Marutians escaped Muirk without incident. When they reached the outskirts, Fendar announced a change of plan. He gave the command for them to follow the road to the west, toward Gotthard, rather than the one north, which would take them directly to Marus. This started a debate with Regmund and Jakin, who thought the trade route due north would be the fastest and easiest way to go.

Fendar beckoned the men to silence and explained, "It may seem like the fastest and easiest route, but it keeps us on Palatian ground for more miles than might be safe. If we go toward Gotthard, we will cross the border sooner and be safely away from King Stefan." He then added, "Besides, the Unseen One has commanded that we go northwest."

Regmund looked at a map and suddenly poked a finger at one point. "Has the Unseen One also commanded that we cross the Great Canyon?" he asked sarcastically. "Your route will bring us to a dead end there."

Fendar snatched the map away from Regmund. "We are not following your maps!" he growled. "We are following by obedience!"

The caravan moved forward again. Danny watched the landscape as it slowly went past. His mind wasn't on the scenery, however. He was worried about Michelle.

Nemathes dragged Michelle back to her room and locked her in. Though she had pleaded for him to tell her why he was so angry, he wouldn't answer. She now sat in her room and waited. Every once in a while, she went to the window and looked out at the gardens. It was a beautifully sunny day. *A good day for traveling,* she thought. And then she imagined Danny, Wayne, and the Marutians making their way out of the city.

Later that afternoon, a key jiggled in the lock of Michelle's bedroom door. She went to it quickly, hoping it was Morgon or someone else who might let her out. But it was Nemathes, who entered with a book in his hand. Then King Stefan walked in. He was clearly agitated and looked even worse than he had that morning.

"This had better be important," Stefan cautioned Nemathes. "I'm overwhelmed now."

"Your Highness will want to know what I've learned," Nemathes assured him.

The king didn't seem to pay attention. He didn't acknowledge

Michelle in any way. Instead, he paced around the room, lost in his thoughts. "I rule a fickle people," he complained while he paced. "One minute they want me to stand firm against Fendar, then the next they want me to give him whatever he wants. Now that I've let the Marutians go, I have people complaining about the work that isn't being done. One nobleman dared to call me a coward for acceding to Fendar. Imagine it! After what happened to us last night, he called me a coward! He said that perhaps they should have made *Fendar* the king! Obviously the man didn't suffer any personal losses. But he will. One way or the other, I'm going to have him executed for daring to speak to me in such a way."

"Then you'll have to kill all your noblemen, Sire," Nemathes said. "They all think you've been tricked or put under a spell."

The king stomped his foot angrily. "Don't they know how hard it was for me to give in to Fendar? Don't they realize that I'd like to kill the man this very instant?"

"Sire, please," Nemathes said, trying to get the king back on track. He opened the book to a marked page. "I have spent the entire night going over the Marutian prophecy about all that has happened to us. I've concluded that possibly you *have* been put under a spell or tricked, Sire."

This caught the king's attention. "What!"

"Listen, my king," Nemathes said, and read:

> By the word of a child, the signs will begin.
> By the word of a child, the heart will deny.
> By the word of a child, the clouds will rise.

The king listened, but whatever Nemathes was getting at didn't come clear. "What does it mean?" he asked.

Michelle wasn't sure what Nemathes was talking about, either.

"Fendar's signs came by the word of a child, the boy he had with him."

"Danny?" Michelle interjected.

Nemathes frowned at her interruption and then continued, "By the word of the second child, it says the heart will deny!" Nemathes said this with great significance and then looked to the king for approval.

The king was still confused and grew more impatient. "What are you talking about?"

Nemathes groaned with frustration. "Michelle is the second child! Her purpose was to keep you from yielding to Fendar."

Michelle was speechless, astonished at this news.

The king glared at his adviser. "To keep me from yielding? But wouldn't the Marutian prophecy *want* me to let the Marutians go free? You're not making sense, Nemathes."

"But Sire, it makes perfect sense," Nemathes argued. "She has advised you repeatedly not to give in to Fendar, has she not?"

"Yes, that's been her advice."

"And as a result, Fendar's signs have become more powerful and destructive. Even up to the death of your very own son!"

The king scowled at Nemathes for mentioning something so painful.

Nemathes waved the book as if in appeal. "Don't you see? She has purposely duped you into doing exactly what Fendar wanted so he could destroy our nation with his signs!"

"That's crazy!" Michelle exclaimed.

"Is it?" Nemathes challenged her. "Then why are you

here? What purpose have you played other than to advise the king to go contrary to his own better sense?"

"But I didn't! The king agreed with me on his own!" Michelle insisted.

"Of course he did," Nemathes said. "What else could he do when you put him under a powerful spell?"

"Spell!" Michelle cried.

"Of course, of course," the king decided. He looked at Michelle, his eyes filled with hatred. "You speak the truth as always, Nemathes."

"No!" Michelle pleaded.

"And I have no doubt that Fendar knew this all along," Stefan continued. "He played me for a bigger fool than I could have imagined. Well, he won't get away with it."

"What are you going to do?" Michelle asked.

"Assemble my army! I am going after the Marutians! I will deal with Fendar once and for all!" The king rushed out of the room.

"What about the girl?" Nemathes called.

"Do whatever you want with her!" the king shouted back over his shoulder.

Nemathes smiled viciously at Michelle. "So I will," he said, rubbing his hands together. "So I will."

CHAPTER FIFTEEN

———◆———

The Great Canyon served as part of the natural border between Palatia's west and Gotthard's southeast. It was a chasm more than a mile wide, with thrusting rock formations, a river far below, and trees that covered vast sections like a green cushion. A natural path led steeply down one side to the canyon floor below, and then it cut across the river and up the other side. While it had taken the Marutians eight hours to reach the canyon itself, Fendar speculated that it would take 10 to 12 hours to get down to the bottom, and another 12 to 14 to get across the river and up the other side.

Fendar sent a messenger ahead, not only to test the trail, but also to assure the king of Gotthard that this massive group of people coming his way was not an invading army from King Stefan. The Gotthardites had always been on good terms with the Marutians. Their relationship with Palatia, though, was strained.

The people made camp, ate an early dinner, and then settled down to sleep. Danny and Wayne stayed close to Fendar, Wondrar, and his family. Danny continued to worry about Michelle. Wayne figured Michelle could talk her way out of anything and chose, instead, to worry that he would never get to fulfill his sign. "Once we cross the canyon, it'll be easy going," he moped. "They won't need me to do anything."

"You're such a meathead," Danny chastised him. "Don't you realize that the sign *has* to be fulfilled? It's not an optional extra."

Wayne took a little comfort from Danny's words, but it didn't stop him from complaining that he had to wait so long.

A buzz filled the camp the next morning as Danny woke

up. He'd slept comfortably in the back of the wagon in a makeshift sleeping bag. He yawned and stretched and immediately noticed that people were up and talking. Wondrar walked past. "What's wrong?" Danny asked.

"There is a rumor going around that King Stefan and his army are on their way to attack us," Wondrar reported.

Danny sat up. "Attack us? But he let us go!" he protested.

Wondrar shrugged and walked on. "I guess he changed his mind."

Within an hour, the rumor had been confirmed as fact by Jakin's scouts. King Stefan and his best cavalrymen were racing in their direction. The entire Palatian army followed behind. They were coming to retrieve the Marutians and kill Fendar.

Danny found Fendar at a campfire, discussing the situation with Regmund, Jakin, and the other elders.

"We're pinned against the edge of a canyon!" Regmund complained. "They'll either trap us or drive us over to our deaths! We're doomed no matter how you look at it."

Fendar sighed wearily. "Have faith for once!" he admonished. "We must keep calm. The Unseen One wouldn't have brought us here to die."

"*You* brought us here, Fendar," another elder said accusingly. "We don't know that this was the Unseen One's plan."

"*Everything* is according to His plan," Fendar snapped at him. "You have to trust in Him."

Wondrar tapped his brother on the shoulder. "I think you should address the people," he suggested. "They are worrying and complaining. Some are already talking about giving themselves up to King Stefan."

"Oh, these children!" Fendar groaned. "Tell everyone to gather around the large oak tree—there in the middle of the field—in one hour."

By the time the people had assembled, most of the Marutians were afraid. King Stefan and his troops were coming closer by the minute. Several of Jakin's men, who had climbed to the top of a nearby hillside, claimed to be able to see the dust from the horses' hooves in the distance.

"People of Marus," Fendar called out from atop a wagon that had been placed under the tree. "Listen to me! The Unseen One has us held firmly in His grip. His hand reaches out to us, to hold us as a father holds a small baby. We must trust and obey Him."

"But what about King Stefan?" someone from the audience shouted.

"We must give up!" another said.

"Better to die in our homes in Muirk than out here in the middle of nowhere!" still another called.

"Don't be afraid," Fendar said to them. "The Unseen One will rescue us."

"How?" many of the Marutians demanded to know. "We'll never get across the canyon in time unless we learn to fly!"

"Do I have to remind you of the signs that the great voices of the past have told us about? According to their words, three children came to us to fulfill three of the signs. You yourself witnessed the signs against the Palatians, brought about by the first child. *This* child." Here he gestured to Danny. "And we know, by King Stefan's actions and how his heart was hardened against us, that the second sign has been fulfilled by the second child."

"Michelle," Danny acknowledged softly and wondered afresh if she were all right.

"But there remains a final sign, a demonstration of the power of the Unseen One by the third child." Fendar waved a hand toward Wayne, who now looked at him bug-eyed.

"Me? Are you sure?" he gulped.

Danny smiled at his brother. His moment had come, and he wasn't ready for it.

"By the word of a child, the clouds will rise," Fendar said, repeating the prophecy. He drew Wayne to his feet on the wagon and handed him the walking stick.

"What am I supposed to do?" Wayne asked nervously.

"Speak the word while you hold up the walking stick," he replied. "The Unseen One has decreed that the sign will not come unless you bring it."

"Boy, I never got to hold the walking stick," Danny teased.

"Be quiet," Wayne said. He asked Fendar, "Uh, what word am I supposed to say?"

Fendar smiled down at the boy. "Rise."

"Rise?"

"Lift up the walking stick and say, 'Rise.'"

With shaking hands and knocking knees, Wayne held up the walking stick. "Rise," he croaked.

"Say it again, louder," Fendar instructed him.

Wayne cleared his throat and then shouted, "Rise!"

"Now," Fendar called out, "come to the edge of the canyon!"

The massive throng followed Fendar, Wayne, Danny, and Wondrar to the cliff that overlooked the canyon. At first there didn't seem to be anything to see.

"Maybe it didn't work," Wayne worried.

"Watch," Fendar said.

Slowly, almost imperceptibly, the floor of the canyon seemed to fade. It looked at first like an optical illusion. The sliver of river disappeared, then the trees.

"It's a rising mist!" someone said and pointed.

Sure enough, a mist covered the bottom of the canyon and

rose up the sides, filling it as if it were being poured in like milk. Then the mist thickened and climbed upward more quickly, swirling and spinning like a storm-tossed sea.

Everyone watched with amazement as the mist rose until it was perfectly level with the edges of the canyon, where it stopped. It stretched from one side to the other like a great, gray desert.

"What good is this?" Regmund asked Fendar. "It looks astonishing, but what help is it to us?"

"We will cross the canyon *on* the cloud!" Fendar announced.

The Marutians reacted with utter disbelief. "It can't be done!" they cried.

"Better to stay here and take our chances with King Stefan!" some said.

"You'll find out the truth of your statement soon enough, for he'll be here before the end of the day," Fendar reminded them.

Regmund looked into the deep, gray swirl. "But how do we know it'll hold us?" he asked.

"It is a matter of faith," Fendar replied. "Do you believe in the Unseen One or don't you?"

"Yes, but . . ." Regmund stepped back from the cliff.

"Who will go first?" Fendar asked.

Everyone stood away from the cliff. Then they began to argue over who should be the first to test the cloud. Fendar watched sadly as they bickered.

Wondrar joined his brother and said, "Maybe I should go first."

"No," Fendar said. "These poor children must take their first baby steps to freedom."

One of Jakin's scouts pushed through the crowd. He was covered in dust and sweat. "King Stefan is approaching!" he reported. "By my guess, he's only a couple of hours away!"

The news moved through the crowd like an earthquake.

"It will take at least that long to get everyone across!" Regmund shouted at Fendar.

"Then I suggest everyone should quit *talking* about crossing and take your step of faith *now*."

The crowd continued to jabber at one another, but no one moved.

"Oh, brother!" Danny said impatiently as he stepped forward. "*I'll* go."

Suddenly Wayne was at his side. "No. I'll go first," he said firmly.

Danny was surprised.

"You *always* get to go first," Wayne explained playfully.

Danny hesitated. What if Fendar was wrong? What if the cloud wouldn't hold him? What would he say to his parents about their youngest son falling to his death? How would Danny cope with the loss of this brother who drove him crazy—yet whom he loved as much as himself?

Wayne tugged at his arm insistently. "Besides, it's *my* cloud. I should go."

Danny very nearly said no. His instincts were to wrap his arms around his brother and drag him back. But before he could do or say anything else, Wayne stepped off the edge of the cliff.

CHAPTER SIXTEEN

Michelle sat at the bottom of the large cage that hung in Nemathes's dungeon. She had wondered before why he had a man-sized birdcage, and now she knew. It was a prison. Rusted manacles hung loose from the bars. Hugging herself in the center of the cage, she tried to keep from touching the grimy bars or the moldy straw that covered the bottom. The cage creaked and swayed any time she moved. She dared not imagine what other creatures had been locked in here, for how long, or for what purposes. The dungeon's dampness seemed to penetrate her very bones. She had been in there for hours.

"Help!" she called out. She didn't really think anyone would come, but it comforted her to hear her own voice.

What a terrible turn of events, she thought. *I lived in a palace and was a counselor to the king. Now look at me. Imprisoned in a cage in a magician's dungeon—a magician who thinks of me as some kind of spellbinding witch. How did it all go wrong?* She frowned as she thought, *I chose the wrong side, that's how. Danny and Wayne were right all along.*

Thinking of the two boys made her wonder where they were at that very moment. Would the king catch up to them, or had they already crossed the border to freedom? Maybe they had already been whisked back to Odyssey—back *home.*

Her eyes welled up with tears as she thought about it. She'd made all the wrong choices and done all the wrong things, and now she was paying the price. Looking at the bars of the cage, she realized she might never be free again, might never go home. The loneliness of it all overwhelmed her.

"I'm sorry," she whispered. She didn't know who she was talking to at first. It might have been Danny and Wayne, since she had been working so hard against them. But in her mind, she pictured Fendar and the walking stick with the power of the Unseen One. "I'm sorry," she said again.

The signs went through her mind, one after the other. She remembered how each one was supposed to persuade the king to change his stubborn heart. *It was my heart that needed to be changed,* Michelle suddenly thought. *I was as stubborn as the king. I always have been.* "I'm sorry," she said once again, and this time she felt as if she were speaking to the Unseen One Himself.

The heavy door leading into the dungeon groaned. Nemathes pushed it open and raced in, his robes billowing as if he were flying. He muttered to himself as he looked around. Then he went to a potbellied stove off to the corner and stoked the dying fire inside. He threw a cup of some kind of powder onto the coals, and they burst instantly to white-hot life. He picked up a long, iron rod, like a poker, and placed one end of it into the coals.

"Yes, yes," he said as he searched for something on the tabletops and in a few of the drawers in the wooden cabinets. "Ah!" he said as he plucked up a few items and took them to his laboratory table. He set a large bowl in the center and dropped the items in. Then he poured in a large container of greenish liquid from one of the beakers.

"Nemathes," Michelle entreated him.

He busied himself with the bowl but said, "It's all so clear to me now, the way you cast your spell."

"But I didn't!" Michelle insisted.

Nemathes didn't listen. "You insinuated yourself into the king's life, his family, his very soul." He turned to her. "You enjoyed the power, didn't you? You were probably one of those apprentice magicians who always dreamed of having great power. I've seen the type before. One whiff of it and you go mad, like a shark to the blood."

"It's not true!" Michelle cried. "I'm not a magician! And I never dreamed of having any power!"

"You lie!" he shouted. "It's written all over your face! You like to be in charge. You want to control others."

"All right, all right!" Michelle conceded. "But I know better now. Honest, I do."

Nemathes continued talking as he worked. "Power is not a child's toy. It carries a terrible burden of responsibility. Do you think I don't have power? More power than the king, let me tell you. But I restrain myself. I understand that power is not to be tinkered with or unleashed, but mastered and *used.* Years ago, I vowed my talents and services to King Akaron and to his son, King Stefan. But tell me, who is *your* master? Fendar? Did he instruct you?"

"No! I never met Fendar until he came to the palace," Michelle said. Then she begged, "You have to let me go. *Please* let me go!"

"I'm afraid you won't be going anywhere. This is your home now." Nemathes gestured to the dungeon. "You will be *my* apprentice now. My slave."

"But you can't! I'm not a slave! I'm free!"

"Freedom is an illusion, you foolish girl. Freedom is simply changing from one master to another. Fendar was your master, and now I am your master." Nemathes closed his eyes and waved his hands over the large bowl as he muttered something. Then he went to Michelle's cage and undid the padlock. He opened the door.

Michelle sat where she was. "What are you going to do to me?" she asked.

"I'm going to show you something. Don't be shy. Come along."

"Is it going to hurt?"

"*I'm* not going to hurt you, if that's what you mean. I want you to see what will become of your friends."

This piqued Michelle's interest. "Danny and Wayne?"

"Yes. I have conjured up a bowl of sight. I want you to see how the king deals with those who defy him."

Michelle climbed out of the cage and stumbled against Nemathes. Her legs had nearly gone to sleep. He steadied her and led her to the table. "We'll watch together, shall we?"

With a careful eye on Nemathes, in case he might be playing a trick, Michelle climbed up on one of the stools and looked into the large bowl. At first she didn't see anything but a greenish, murky fluid.

"The picture has gone all fuzzy," Nemathes said. He waved his hand over the bowl again.

As if watching a television that had just come on, Michelle could see a picture of hundreds of people walking. They were all going in the same direction, from a large, brown patch of land onto a whitish-gray sand that looked like steam, and then across to another brown patch.

"The Marutians," Nemathes stated.

Michelle was mystified. "How can we see this?"

"Through the eyes of Excelsior, my eagle. He is flying around the site."

Michelle adjusted her glasses to make sure she wasn't imagining what she was seeing. "What are they doing?"

Nemathes looked closer and gasped, "They seem to be crossing the Great Canyon from Palatia to Gotthard! But by what dark arts? There is no bridge there, and yet they walk freely across the top!"

By no spoken command, the eagle circled in closer. "What is it?" Nemathes mumbled.

Closer now, the whitish-gray sand seemed to be swirling and spinning beneath the feet of the Marutians. Michelle still couldn't see what it was.

"It is a cloud!" Nemathes suddenly shouted. Michelle couldn't tell if he was alarmed or impressed. "They are crossing the Great Canyon on a cloud!"

"By the word of a child, the clouds will rise," Michelle remembered aloud.

The eagle then flew higher and higher and looked back in the direction from which the Marutians had come. In the far distance, men on horseback raced toward the canyon. It was the king and his cavalry.

Michelle felt a tightness in her chest. A large group of the Marutians was still moving onto the cloud from the Palatian side. She wanted to shout, to warn them.

"It's only a matter of time," Nemathes observed.

From the eagle's vantage point, they could see the king's horsemen getting closer and closer. The Marutians who'd taken up the rear also saw them and, panicked, now rushed onto the cloud. *They're not going to make it*, Michelle thought.

The edge of the cloud on the Palatian side seemed to move. First it spilled over, like bony fingers tentatively touching the land. Then it reached over fully and spread across the land toward the coming cavalry. As fast as the horses came in one direction, the cloud moved more swiftly in the other. Michelle braced herself for a terrible head-on collision between the two.

"No!" Nemathes screamed. "Beware, Sire, beware!"

By now, the king and his men saw the coming cloud and began to slow down. The cloud didn't hit or crush them but moved through them like a normal mist. It was thick enough, though, to keep the king and his cavalry from advancing. They had no choice but to wait.

Nemathes could hardly contain his anger.

Michelle sat back, relieved that the Marutians had this chance to escape. The last of them quickly made their way across the canyon to the other side. Michelle could see Fendar and Wondrar now, standing at the edge of the cliff. Danny and Wayne were next to them. She felt a sad sense of regret. She should have been with them.

Once the last of the Marutians had their feet placed solidly on the Gotthard side, Wondrar held up the walking stick and waved it three times.

"What's this?" Nemathes hissed.

The mist around the king's horsemen suddenly lifted and faded, as if it had never been there. King Stefan commanded his men to go forward.

"No, Sire, it must be some sort of trick!" Nemathes called to the bowl. But the king obviously couldn't hear him and raced onward.

Michelle wondered what kind of trick it could be. It looked to her as if the king and his cavalry could easily reach the Marutians by crossing the cloud.

The king's horses sped to the edge of the cliff but then suddenly drew to a halt at the risen cloud. Clearly, the horses' instincts told them not to go on.

"Thank the gods for the wisdom of beasts," Nemathes said.

King Stefan turned to his men, and Michelle guessed they were arguing about whether to cross. She knew what they were saying. It still looked like a cloud, they reasoned, and yet an entire nation of people had just crossed on it. Should they go on or shouldn't they?

"Stop where you are!" Nemathes begged them. "It's no use now."

The eagle must have called or screeched, because King Stefan looked up at it. He pointed, as if he recognized the eagle.

Nemathes was delighted. "Yes, Sire, you know me. Now heed my warning. Turn back. Don't trust any of Fendar's magic!"

But the appearance of the eagle seemed to have the opposite effect on the king.

"He thinks it's a sign!" Michelle blurted out. "He thinks your eagle wants them to go on!"

The king commanded his men to spur their horses forward.

Nemathes grabbed the edge of the bowl. "Don't do it, my king! Don't!"

But the king's cavalry went on, spurring and whipping the horses until they abandoned their natural instincts and stepped out onto the cloud. Like a miracle, it held them! They could cross just as the Marutians had!

"Is it possible?" Nemathes asked, daring to hope again that his king might succeed.

On the Gotthard side, the Marutians were in a terrible state of panic. Most of them dropped their things and tore away from the canyon, running wildly across the vast plain. Fendar, Wondrar, Danny, Wayne, and only a handful of others remained on the canyon's edge.

"What kind of trick is this?" Nemathes said. "Why would Fendar allow King Stefan to cross?"

The entire cavalry was on the cloud now, dashing closer and closer to Fendar.

"Why does he stand there?" Nemathes wondered. "Why doesn't he run?"

The answer came when King Stefan, in the lead, was only a few yards away. The cloud suddenly billowed up and seemed to blow away from under the horses' hooves. King Stefan and his men sank into it, slowly at first, as if they'd been caught in quicksand.

"No!" Nemathes shrieked.

Then, as if someone had opened a trap door, the men and their horses disappeared into the thick, white cloud. A moment later, the cloud dissipated to reveal the open space of the canyon floor. There was no doubt that the king and his men lay dead somewhere below.

Nemathes's face was red with a quivering fury unlike anything Michelle had ever seen. He swung around to her, his hand lashing out. It caught her on the side of the head and sent her sprawling backward off the stool and onto the floor. Though her head buzzed, Michelle crawled away as quickly as she could.

Nemathes came toward her. "You have killed my king!" he screamed.

Michelle climbed quickly to her feet and dashed for the door. Nemathes caught her by the collar, spun her around, and threw her into the shelves of books. Something scratched at her forehead, and the wind was knocked out of her as she collapsed in a gasping heap against the wall.

"You cannot live now!" Nemathes said as he came at her. He could easily have grabbed her, but off to his right, the bowl of sight suddenly made a strange popping sound, and then a mist—like the one they had seen at the canyon—blew into the room like smoke from a chimney. In no time at all, it enveloped Nemathes until he was an obscure shadow. The table, the wooden cabinets, and the rest of the room soon faded. Then all was dead quiet.

Once Michelle got her breath back, she pulled herself up. She touched the scratch on her forehead and saw blood on her fingers. She had to make her way to the door, she knew. But would Nemathes reach out and grab her as she passed?

Through the mist, Michelle saw what looked like the red glow of a fire. Was it the potbellied stove? Hoping it would give her a sense of direction for the room—and how to reach the door—she went toward it. It crackled pleasantly. She then realized two things. First, it wasn't the fire in the potbellied stove. This was a large, *open* fire. Before she could panic at the thought of being trapped by a fire in the dungeon, she realized the second thing: Her clothes were soaking wet.

CHAPTER SEVENTEEN

—◆————◆—

"Now we may find our freedom," Wondrar said as he looked down into the canyon.

"Now we may go *home*," Fendar added.

Danny and Wayne, dumbfounded by everything that had happened, moved away from the edge of the Great Canyon. "Whoa!" Wayne said softly.

"Gather the people and tell them to camp here," Fendar told his brother. "We will worship and celebrate what the Unseen One has done for us."

Before he went, Wondrar embraced Danny and then Wayne. The boys were confused, but he left before they could ask why he'd done that.

Danny felt a little light-headed. Was it his imagination, or was the mist still moving around them?

"The signs are fulfilled," Fendar informed the boys. "More will come to us by other means as we make our way home, but you have done all you were called to do."

"You mean we're done?" Wayne asked.

"Yes."

"But I wanted to see Marus," Danny said.

Fendar held up his arms. "It's a long journey, one you can't take. You have journeys of your own. You must go home now."

Danny felt the sting of disappointment.

Wayne, surprisingly, sounded enthusiastic. "How will we go back?" he asked. "Do we have to go back to the fountain?"

Even as he asked the question, the mist grew thicker around them both. Fendar, who was only a few feet away, started to blur.

Danny realized what was happening and reached out to touch Fendar. He wanted to shake his hand, hug him, or do *something* to say thanks for their adventure. Fendar reached toward him as well, and their fingertips brushed quickly.

"Good-bye, and thank *you*," Fendar said, as if from a long way off.

"It's too fast!" Danny said to Wayne as the cloud surrounded them like a blanket.

Wayne suddenly sniffed and observed, "I smell smoke."

So did Danny. Then they heard the crackling of a large fire and the press of warmth on their backs. They turned to see a large bonfire several feet away.

"Where did that come from?" Danny asked.

They both moved toward the fire, their clothes and sneakers slopping wet on the ground.

Looking at each other, they pointed and burst into laughter. "You're soaked!" they said in unison.

"Strange, isn't it?" a familiar voice said. It was Michelle. She was wrapped in a blanket and stood next to the fire. At the sight of her, the mist suddenly cleared. They were at Trickle Lake again. The police had rounded up everyone who'd fallen into the lake and were letting them dry by the fire.

"There was no need for a riot," one of the officers said to a college student.

"You *scared* us, man!" the young man replied.

"Are you all right?" Danny asked Michelle.

She pulled her glasses down her nose a little and pointed to her forehead. "I think I banged it on one of the boats."

"But what happened to you? How did you get back?"

Michelle looked around self-consciously and whispered, "Let's talk about it later. I don't want anyone to think we're crazy."

Danny understood and nodded. He had a strong feeling it would be better if they *never* talked about what had happened, except among themselves.

"I have something to say now, though," Michelle said. "And I'd better say it before I change my mind."

"When do you ever change your mind?" Wayne teased.

Michelle smiled.

"We'll talk about *everything* later," Danny said, letting her off the hook for the moment. For one reason or another, they all had apologies to make.

"You kids are free to go home," a policeman told the three of them.

Grateful they weren't going to be arrested, they headed for their bikes after Michelle gave back the officer's blanket.

"Those are two words I'll never forget," Michelle said as they climbed onto their High Flyers.

"What two words?" Danny asked.

"*Free* and *home*," she replied and pedaled away.

The boys, realizing she intended to race them back, took off after her.

EPILOGUE

A heavy knock sounded on the door to James Curtis's apartment. It startled Whit and the reporter, and they looked up from their respective manuscripts. Mrs. Delullo peered in. "The doctor says you have to leave now," she informed them.

Whit nodded and stood up. The reporter hesitated for a moment, as if he were trying to think of a way to stay a little longer. He gave up and grabbed his coat.

Whit asked the nurse, "If you can't find Mr. Curtis, what will you do with his things?"

She shrugged. "Box it all up and put it away somewhere until we can figure out who to leave it with," she said.

Whit frowned. "That would be a shame. Tell the doctor that I'd be happy to store Mr. Curtis's things." He tapped the top of the manuscript he'd just read. "I have a home for these at the Whit's End library if he's interested."

"That's only if we can't find Mr. Curtis," the nurse reminded him. "James Curtis is *missing*. We don't assume he's dead. We'll find him."

Whit and the reporter exchanged a knowing glance. They both had a nagging suspicion that they wouldn't be seeing James Curtis again.

Outside, the snow had stopped, but a cold wind remained. The reporter was about to go to his car, but he paused and asked Whit, "Has James Curtis run away, or has he gone back to Marus?"

Whit shrugged. "I wouldn't venture a guess."

"Neither would I," the reporter agreed.

Whit pulled on a pair of gloves and looked out at the snow-covered grounds. He wondered about it all.

"Mr. Whittaker, would you mind telling me *everything* you know about the Marus manuscripts?" the reporter inquired. "I'd like to get all this from the very beginning."

Whit thought it was a good idea. "Let's call Jack Allen," he suggested. "He found the first manuscript in the bottom of an old trunk. That's where it all started."

Whit and the reporter drove back to Odyssey. They later met Jack for a meal and a long conversation.

The reporter sat down at the table in his hotel room, a cup of tea in his hand. He sipped the drink and frowned. It was nasty-tasting stuff. He'd just made it from a tea bag in the small pot provided by the hotel. Somewhere outside, the wind howled in the darkness. The weather report was calling for more snow.

The reporter expected to be stuck in Odyssey for a few days at least.

He turned on his laptop computer, the screen flickered, and the hard drive made a buzzing noise at him as it came to life. He glanced at the scattered notes he'd scribbled during the day. Whit and Jack had told him quite a story. *This is some mystery,* the reporter thought. *It should stimulate a few healthy debates among our readers.*

But for now, he still had a lot of missing pieces and facts to fill in. And one way or another, he was determined to get copies of all the manuscripts. Tomorrow he'd use all his powers of persuasion on the administrator of Hillingdale Haven.

He took another drink of his tea and knew there'd be many more cups ahead. He began to type:

The winter rain fell like cold splinters on Odyssey. John Avery Whittaker, or Whit as he is best known, stood at the front window of Whit's End, his popular soda shop and discovery emporium. He watched the drops hit the grass that stretched out to the street. Cars splashed past. Men and women with large overcoats and billowing umbrellas crouched as they walked up and down the sidewalk. The grayness washed all color out of the day.

I won't get a lot of kids asking for ice cream today, he said to himself. He decided to get out an extra supply of hot chocolate mix.

One man suddenly ducked from the main street and made his way up the sidewalk to the front door of the shop. He burrowed deep into his coat to brace himself against the rain. One hand struggled with an umbrella. His other hand clutched a large, brown envelope. Whit smiled. It was Jack Allen. ...